Kaplan Publishing are constantly finding new ways to support students looking for exam success and our online resources really do add an extra dimension to your studies.

This book comes with free MyKaplan online resources so that you can study anytime, anywhere. **This free online resource is not sold separately and is included in the price of the book.**

Having purchased this book, you have access to the following online study materials:

CONTENT	AAT	
	Text	Kit
Electronic version of the book	✓	✓
Knowledge Check tests with instant answers	✓	
Mock assessments online	✓	✓
Material updates	✓	✓

How to access your online resources

Received this book as part of your Kaplan course?
If you have a MyKaplan account, your full online resources will be added automatically, in line with the information in your course confirmation email. If you've not used MyKaplan before, you'll be sent an activation email once your resources are ready.

Bought your book from Kaplan?
We'll automatically add your online resources to your MyKaplan account. If you've not used MyKaplan before, you'll be sent an activation email.

Bought your book from elsewhere?
Go to **www.mykaplan.co.uk/add-online-resources**
Enter the ISBN number found on the title page and back cover of this book.
Add the unique pass key number contained in the scratch panel below.
You may be required to enter additional information during this process to set up or confirm your account details.

This code can only be used once for the registration of this book online. This registration and your online content will expire when the examinations covered by this book have taken place. Please allow one hour from the time you submit your book details for us to process your request.

Please scratch the film to access your unique code.

Please be aware that this code is case-sensitive and you will need to include the dashes within the passcode, but not when entering the ISBN.

AAT

Q2022

Principles of Costing

EXAM KIT

This Exam Kit supports study for the following AAT qualifications:

AAT Level 2 Certificate in Accounting

AAT Level 2 Certificate in Bookkeeping

AAT Certificate in Accounting at SCQF Level 6

British Library Cataloguing-in-Publication Data

A catalogue record for this book is available from the British Library.

Published by:

Kaplan Publishing UK

Unit 2 The Business Centre

Molly Millar's Lane

Wokingham

Berkshire

RG41 2QZ

ISBN: 978-1-83996-887-7

© Kaplan Financial Limited, 2024

Printed and bound in Great Britain.

The text in this material and any others made available by any Kaplan Group company does not amount to advice on a particular matter and should not be taken as such. No reliance should be placed on the content as the basis for any investment or other decision or in connection with any advice given to third parties. Please consult your appropriate professional adviser as necessary. Kaplan Publishing Limited and all other Kaplan group companies expressly disclaim all liability to any person in respect of any losses or other claims, whether direct, indirect, incidental, consequential or otherwise arising in relation to the use of such materials.

All rights reserved. No part of this examination may be reproduced or transmitted in any form or by any means, electronic or mechanical, including photocopying, recording, or by any information storage and retrieval system, without prior permission from Kaplan Publishing.

CONTENTS

	Page
Unit-specific information	P.4
Index to questions and answers	P.5
Exam technique	P.10
Kaplan's recommended revision approach	P.11

Practice questions	1
Answers to practice questions	63
Mock – questions	111
Mock – answers	121

Features in this exam kit

In addition to providing a wide ranging bank of real exam style questions, we have also included in this kit:

- unit-specific information and advice on exam technique
- our recommended approach to make your revision for this particular unit as effective as possible.

You will find a wealth of other resources to help you with your studies on the AAT website:

www.aat.org.uk/

Quality and accuracy are of the utmost importance to us so if you spot an error in any of our products, please send an email to mykaplanreporting@kaplan.com with full details, or follow the link to the feedback form in MyKaplan.

Our Quality Co-ordinator will work with our technical team to verify the error and take action to ensure it is corrected in future editions.

UNIT-SPECIFIC INFORMATION

THE EXAM

FORMAT OF THE ASSESSMENT

The assessment will comprise seven independent tasks. Learners will be assessed by computer-based assessment.

In any one assessment, learners may not be assessed on all content, or on the full depth or breadth of a piece of content. The content assessed may change over time to ensure validity of assessment, but all assessment criteria will be tested over time.

The learning outcomes for this unit are as follows:

	Learning outcome	Weighting
1	Understand the cost recording system within an organisation	30%
2	Use cost recording techniques	40%
3	Provide information on actual and budgeted costs and income	20%
4	Use tools and techniques to support cost calculations	10%
	Total	100%

Time allowed

90 minutes

PASS MARK

The pass mark for all AAT CBAs is 70%.

 Always keep your eye on the clock and make sure you attempt all questions!

DETAILED SYLLABUS

The detailed syllabus and study guide written by the AAT can be found at:

www.aat.org.uk/

INDEX TO QUESTIONS AND ANSWERS

		Page number	
		Question	Answer
COST CLASSIFICATION			
Financial and Management Accounting			
1	FAMA	1	63
2	Financial and management	1	63
3	MAFA	2	64
4	Features	2	64
Responsibility centres			
5	Mariam	2	64
6	Print plc	3	64
7	Hooch plc	3	65
8	Swing plc	4	65
Classifying costs by element (materials, labour or overheads)			
9	VVV Ltd	4	66
10	Trip Ltd	4	66
11	FRUWT Ltd	5	66
12	Martina	5	66
Classifying costs by nature (direct or indirect)			
13	Khaled	5	67
14	Russett Ltd	6	67
15	Scotland Ltd	6	67
16	Direct or Indirect	6	67
17	Direct costs	6	67
Classifying costs by function (production, administration or selling and distribution)			
18	Noogle Ltd	7	68
19	Heaving Ltd	7	68
20	Korma plc	7	68
21	Petar	8	69
Classifying costs by behaviour (fixed, variable or semi-variable)			
22	Quark Ltd	8	69
23	Morn Ltd	8	69
24	Stepped fixed cost	9	69
25	Braetak Ltd	9	70
26	Odo Ltd	9	70
27	Definitions	10	70
28	Match a graph	10	70

AAT: PRINCIPLES OF COSTING

		Page number	
		Question	Answer
COST CODING			
29	Bytes Ltd	11	71
30	Hero Ltd	11	71
31	Villain Ltd	12	71
32	Nayulz Ltd	13	71
33	Jumper Ltd	13	72
34	Greenfingers	14	72
COST BEHAVIOUR			
Calculation questions			
35	Hulk plc	15	72
36	Banner plc	15	73
37	Norton plc	16	73
38	Triumph Ltd	16	73
39	Youngs Ltd	16	74
40	Care plc	17	74
41	Robshaw Ltd	17	74
Narrative style questions			
42	Bungle Ltd	17	75
43	TF	18	75
44	Fixed or variable	18	75
45	FOV	18	75
46	VOF	18	75
47	Storm	19	76
48	Rogue	19	76
49	Gambit	19	76
Cost cards, total costs and unit costs			
50	Jeepers Ltd	20	77
51	Braniac Ltd	20	77
52	Marko Ltd	21	77
53	Bizarro Ltd	21	78
54	Vinny Ltd	22	78
55	Darkseid Ltd	22	78
56	Olsen Ltd	23	78
57	Flakeaway Ltd	23	79
58	Coronation Ltd	24	79
59	Luthor Ltd	24	79
Overhead absorption			
60	Wilkinson Ltd	25	80
61	Hodgson Ltd	26	80
62	Barnes Ltd	27	81
63	Maja Ltd	27	81

INDEX TO QUESTIONS AND ANSWERS

		Page number	
		Question	Answer
Manufacturing Accounts			
64	Joker Ltd	28	82
65	Tut Ltd	29	83
66	Riddler Ltd	30	84
67	Clocking Ltd	31	84
68	Bookworm Ltd	32	85
69	Multi	32	85
COSTING FOR INVENTORY AND WORK-IN-PROGRESS			
Narrative style questions			
70	Bobble Ltd	33	85
71	Lint Ltd	33	85
72	Fluff Ltd	34	86
73	Fido Ltd	34	86
74	Truffeaux Ltd	34	86
75	Stocky Ltd	35	86
76	Buffer	35	87
77	Inventory	35	87
Identification of inventory valuation method			
78	Epic Ltd	36	87
79	Awesome Ltd	37	88
80	Amazing Ltd	37	89
Inventory cards			
81	Stone Ltd	38	90
82	Natal Ltd	38	90
83	Gandalf Ltd	39	90
84	Grundy Ltd	39	91
85	Lobo Ltd	40	91
86	Zod Ltd	40	92
COSTING FOR LABOUR			
Narrative-style questions			
87	Nulab Ltd	41	93
88	Lu Ltd	41	93
89	Mandela Ltd	41	93
90	Perres Ltd	42	93
91	Tevez Ltd	42	94
92	Berdych Ltd	42	94
93	Soderling Ltd	43	94
94	Murray Ltd	43	94
95	Olga Ltd	43	94
96	Piecework Statements	44	95

KAPLAN PUBLISHING

		Page number	
		Question	Answer
Calculating labour costs			
97	Mutant Ltd	44	95
98	Phoenix Ltd	44	95
99	Kahn Ltd	45	96
100	Enterprise Ltd	45	96
101	SGC Ltd	45	96
102	Gothic Ltd	46	97
103	Avengers Ltd	46	97
104	Draco Ltd	46	97
105	Quagga plc	47	98
106	JLA plc	47	98
107	Injustice Ltd	47	98
108	Greenwood Ltd	48	98
109	Sancho Ltd	48	98
BUDGETING AND VARIANCES			
Narrative questions			
110	Pierre Ltd	49	99
111	Nixon Ltd	49	99
112	Various Ltd	49	99
113	Noor Ltd	50	100
114	Gatland Ltd	50	100
115	Lancaster Ltd	51	101
116	Goode Ltd	51	101
117	Brown Ltd	52	101
118	Magenta Ltd	52	101
119	Carlota Ltd	52	102
Calculation questions			
120	Funky Ltd	53	102
121	Erebor Ltd	53	102
122	Moria Ltd	54	103
123	Wyedale Ltd	54	103
124	Belegost Ltd	55	103
125	Ivan Ltd	55	104
126	Bluebell Ltd	56	104
127	Telmah Ltd	56	105

INDEX TO QUESTIONS AND ANSWERS

		Page number	
		Question	**Answer**
SPREADSHEETS			
128	Cells	57	106
129	Doomsday Ltd	57	106
130	Gru Ltd	58	107
131	Herb plc	59	108
132	Kamile Ltd	60	109
133	Phineas Ltd	61	110

MOCK ASSESSMENT		
Questions and answers	111	121

EXAM TECHNIQUE

- **Do not skip any of the material** in the syllabus.

- **Read each question** *very* carefully.

- **Double-check your answer** before committing yourself to it.

- Answer **every** question – if you do not know an answer to a multiple choice question or true/false question, you don't lose anything by guessing. Think carefully before you **guess**.

- If you are answering a multiple-choice question, **eliminate first those answers that you know are wrong.** Then choose the most appropriate answer from those that are left.

- **Don't panic** if you realise you've answered a question incorrectly. Getting one question wrong will not mean the difference between passing and failing.

Computer-based exams – tips

- Do not attempt a CBA until you have **completed all study material** relating to it.

- On the AAT website there is a CBA demonstration. It is **ESSENTIAL** that you attempt this before your real CBA. You will become familiar with how to move around the CBA screens and the way that questions are formatted, increasing your confidence and speed in the actual exam.

- Be sure you understand how to use the **software** before you start the exam. If in doubt, ask the assessment centre staff to explain it to you.

- Questions are **displayed on the screen** and answers are entered using keyboard and mouse. At the end of the exam, you are given a certificate showing the result you have achieved.

- In addition to the traditional multiple-choice question type, CBAs will also contain **other types of questions**, such as number entry questions, drag and drop, true/false, pick lists or drop down menus or hybrids of these.

- In some CBAs you will have to type in complete computations or written answers.

- You need to be sure you **know how to answer questions** of this type before you sit the exam, through practice.

KAPLAN'S RECOMMENDED REVISION APPROACH

QUESTION PRACTICE IS THE KEY TO SUCCESS

Success in professional examinations relies upon you acquiring a firm grasp of the required knowledge at the tuition phase. In order to be able to do the questions, knowledge is essential.

However, the difference between success and failure often hinges on your exam technique on the day and making the most of the revision phase of your studies.

The **Kaplan Study Text** is the starting point, designed to provide the underpinning knowledge to tackle all questions. However, in the revision phase, poring over text books is not the answer.

Kaplan Pocket Notes are designed to help you quickly revise a topic area; however you then need to practise questions. There is a need to progress to exam style questions as soon as possible, and to tie your exam technique and technical knowledge together.

The importance of question practice cannot be over-emphasised.

The recommended approach below is designed by expert tutors in the field, in conjunction with their knowledge of the examiner and the specimen assessment.

You need to practise as many questions as possible in the time you have left.

OUR AIM

Our aim is to get you to the stage where you can attempt exam questions confidently, to time, in a closed book environment, with no supplementary help (i.e. to simulate the real examination experience).

Practising your exam technique is also vitally important for you to assess your progress and identify areas of weakness that may need more attention in the final run up to the examination.

In order to achieve this we recognise that initially you may feel the need to practice some questions with open book help.

Good exam technique is vital.

THE KAPLAN REVISION PLAN

Stage 1: Assess areas of strengths and weaknesses

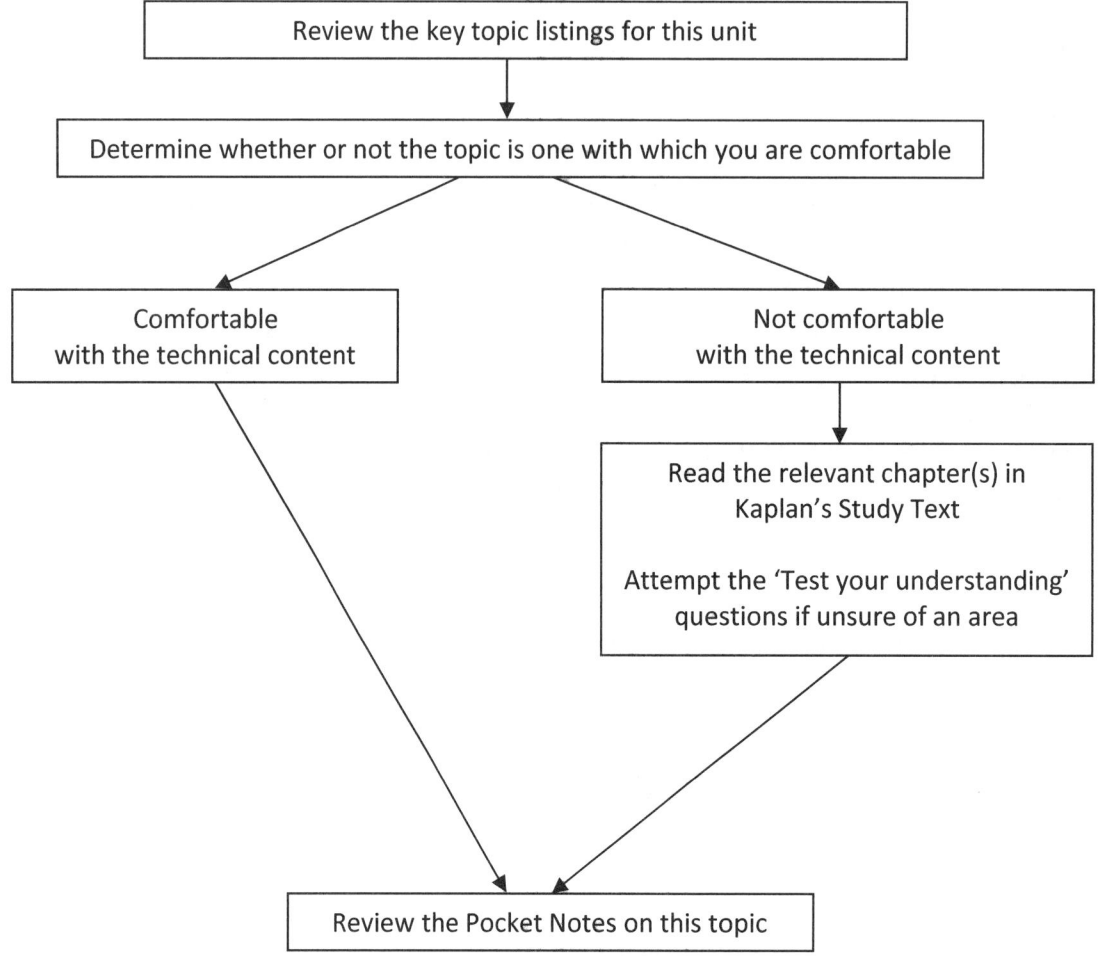

Stage 2: Practice questions

Follow the order of revision of topics as presented in this Kit and attempt the questions in the order suggested.

Try to avoid referring to Study Texts and your notes and the model answer until you have completed your attempt.

Review your attempt with the model answer and assess how much of the answer you achieved.

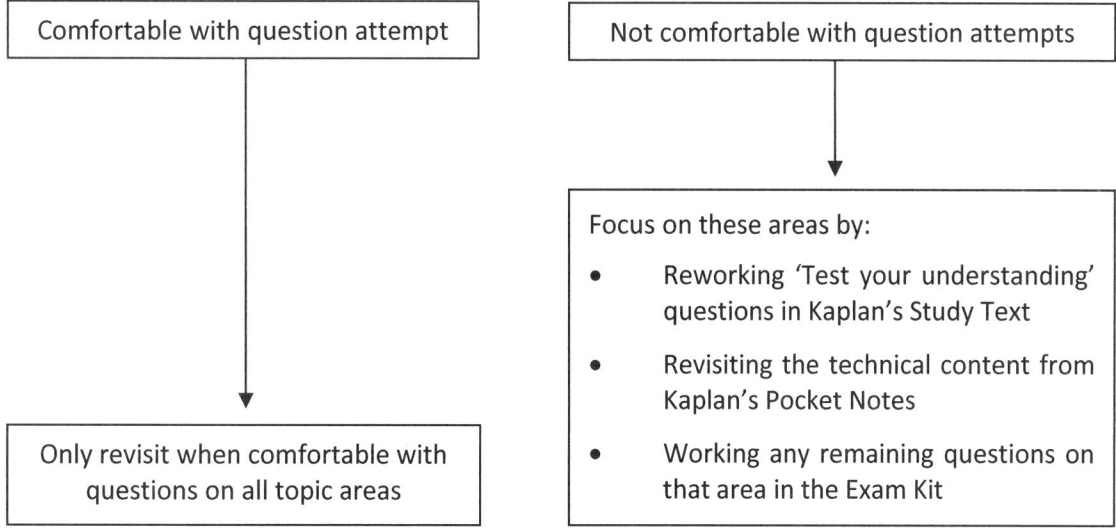

Stage 3: Final pre-exam revision

We recommend that you **attempt at least one mock examination** containing a set of previously unseen exam-standard questions.

Attempt the mock CBA online in timed, closed book conditions to simulate the real exam experience.

Section 1

PRACTICE QUESTIONS

COST CLASSIFICATION

FINANCIAL AND MANAGEMENT ACCOUNTING

1   FAMA

The table below lists some of the characteristics of financial accounting and management accounting systems.

Indicate two characteristics for each system by putting a tick in the relevant column of the table below:

Characteristic	Financial accounting	Management accounting
• Have to be produced annually.		
• Analyses historic events to help produce forecasts.		
• Is always produced using accounting standards.		
• Is produced on an ad hoc basis when required.		

2   FINANCIAL AND MANAGEMENT

The table below lists some of the characteristics of financial accounting and management accounting systems.

Indicate two characteristics for each system by putting a tick in the relevant column of the table below:

Characteristic	Financial accounting	Management accounting
• Must be presented as specified by the Companies Act and accounting standards.		
• Helps managers run the business on a day-to-day basis.		
• Used as the basis for the calculation of the organisation's tax charge.		
• Can include anything that managers feel is useful for the business.		

AAT: PRINCIPLES OF COSTING

3 MAFA

The table below lists some of the characteristics of financial accounting and management accounting systems.

Indicate two characteristics for each system by putting a tick in the relevant column of the table below:

Characteristic	Management accounting	Financial accounting
• It is based on past events.		
• Its purpose is to provide information for managers.		
• It is based on future events.		
• It complies with company law and accounting rules.		

4 FEATURES

The table below lists some features typical of financial accounting and management accounting systems.

Indicate which feature applies to which system by putting a tick in the relevant column of the table below:

Feature	Financial accounting	Management accounting
• Analysis of profit by cost centre.		
• Statement of profit or loss using format as dictated by accounting standards and company law.		
• Cash flow forecasts.		
• Cost per unit calculation.		

RESPONSIBILITY CENTRES

5 MARIAM

Mariam operates a business that bakes bread. These are made in a small bakery and then sent to Mariam's shop, where they are sold. Mariam also has a small office where all of the administration is undertaken.

Identify whether the following departments are likely to be profit or cost centres by putting a tick in the relevant column of the table below:

	Cost centre	Profit centre
• Bakery		
• Shop		
• Office		

6 PRINT PLC

Print plc is a large company that prints and sells books. It is split into three divisions – binding, shops and marketing. The binding department prints the books. These are then either transferred to Print plc's chain of shops where they are sold to the public, or sold direct from the binding department to corporate clients. The marketing department produces all of Print's advertising.

Identify whether the following departments are likely to be profit or cost centres by putting a tick in the relevant column of the table below:

	Cost centre	Profit centre
• Binding		
• Shops		
• Marketing		

7 HOOCH PLC

Identify which type of responsibility centre is being defined by putting a tick in the relevant column of the table below:

	Cost centre	Revenue centre	Profit centre	Investment centre
• Hooch's manager has no responsibility for income or asset purchases and disposals.				
• Hooch's manager is assessed on the profitability of their department, as well as how effectively they have controlled their assets.				
• Hooch's manager is responsible for income and expenditure of their department only.				
• Hooch's manager is responsible for income only.				

8 SWING PLC

Identify which type of responsibility centre is most likely for each of the scenarios in the table below by putting a tick in the relevant column:

	Cost centre	Revenue centre	Profit centre	Investment centre
• HR department.				
• A subsidiary company of a large corporation which makes its own capital investment decisions.				
• Sales department responsible only for meeting sales targets.				
• Individual restaurant in a large chain.				

CLASSIFYING COSTS BY ELEMENT (MATERIALS, LABOUR OR OVERHEADS)

9 VVV LTD

VVV Ltd manufactures toy planes.

Classify the following costs by element by putting a tick in the relevant column of the table below:

Cost	Materials	Labour	Overheads
• Paint used on the planes.			
• Depreciation of the machines used in the factory.			
• Oil used on the machines in the factory.			
• Salary of worker assembling the planes.			

10 TRIP LTD

Trip Ltd is a company that provides travel insurance.

Classify the following costs by element by putting a tick in the relevant column of the table below:

Cost	Materials	Labour	Overheads
• Wages of the insurance clerks dealing with claims.			
• Rent of the office.			
• Paper used to print off insurance policies.			
• Salary of the office manager.			

PRACTICE QUESTIONS: SECTION 1

11 FRUWT LTD

FRUWT Ltd manufactures and sells fruit juice.

Classify the following costs by element by putting a tick in the relevant column of the table below:

Cost	Materials	Labour	Overheads
• Purchase of fruit for juicing.			
• Electricity used by juicing machines.			
• Water added to the juice before sale.			
• Wages of staff operating juicing machinery.			

12 MARTINA

Martina provides legal services in her home town.

Classify the following costs by element by putting a tick in the relevant column of the table below:

Cost	Materials	Labour	Overheads
• Stationery used in Martina's court cases.			
• Wages of Martina's secretary.			
• Water rates for Martina's office.			
• Cost of training courses taken by Martina.			

CLASSIFYING COSTS BY NATURE (DIRECT OR INDIRECT)

13 KHALED

Khaled runs a newspaper.

Classify the following costs by nature by putting a tick in the relevant column of the table below:

Cost	Direct	Indirect
• Paper used in the newspapers.		
• Wages of warehouse staff.		
• Heat and light for head office.		
• Ink used in printing the newspapers.		

14 RUSSETT LTD

Russett Ltd is in business as a tablet computer manufacturer.

Classify the following costs by nature by putting a tick in the relevant column of the table below:

Cost	Direct	Indirect
• Glass used to make tablets.		
• Insurance of factory.		
• Wages of workers assembling tablets.		
• Cost of entertaining corporate clients.		

15 SCOTLAND LTD

Scotland Ltd makes sports clothing.

Classify the following costs by nature by putting a tick in the relevant column of the table below:

Cost	Direct	Indirect
• Cleaners' wages.		
• Advertising expense.		
• Material used in production.		
• Production manager's wages.		
• Machinist wages.		

16 DIRECT OR INDIRECT

Classify the following costs by nature by putting a tick in the relevant column of the table below:

Cost	Direct	Indirect
• Chargeable hour for a lawyer.		
• Machine hire for a building contractor in a long term contract.		
• Electricity for a garden centre.		
• Audit fee for a restaurant.		

17 DIRECT COSTS

Direct costs are conventionally deemed to:

A be constant in total when activity levels alter

B be constant per unit of activity

C vary per unit of activity where activity levels alter

D vary in total when activity levels remain constant

PRACTICE QUESTIONS: SECTION 1

CLASSIFYING COSTS BY FUNCTION (PRODUCTION, ADMINISTRATION OR SELLING AND DISTRIBUTION)

18 NOOGLE LTD

Noogle Ltd produces microwaveable ready meals.

Classify the following costs by function by putting a tick in the relevant column of the table below:

Cost	Production	Administration	Selling and distribution
• Purchases of plastic for ready meal containers.			
• Depreciation of sales department's delivery lorries.			
• Insurance of office computers.			
• Salaries of production workers.			

19 HEAVING LTD

Heaving Ltd produces exercise equipment.

Classify the following costs by function by putting a tick in the relevant column of the table below:

Cost	Production	Administration	Selling and distribution
• Paper used to print off sales invoices.			
• Metal used to make weights and bars.			
• Depreciation of sales person's vehicle.			
• Repairs to machine in factory.			

20 KORMA PLC

Classify the following costs by function by putting a tick in the relevant column of the table below:

Cost	Production	Administration	Selling and distribution	Finance
• Direct materials.				
• Sales director salary.				
• Head office printer ink.				
• Direct labour.				
• Bank charges.				

AAT: PRINCIPLES OF COSTING

21 PETAR

Petar makes false teeth.

Classify the following costs by function by putting a tick in the relevant column of the table below:

Cost	Production	Administration	Selling and distribution	Finance
• Salary of receptionist.				
• Plastic used in false teeth.				
• Stationery provided to all departments.				
• Interest on Petar's bank overdraft.				
• Electricity for Petar's factory.				

CLASSIFYING COSTS BY BEHAVIOUR (FIXED, VARIABLE OR SEMI-VARIABLE)

22 QUARK LTD

Quark Ltd runs a bar.

Classify the following costs by their behaviour by putting a tick in the relevant column of the table below:

Cost	Fixed	Variable	Semi-variable
• Bar manager's salary.			
• Alcohol used to make drinks.			
• Rent of bar.			
• Telephone costs, including standard line rental charge.			

23 MORN LTD

Morn Ltd is a manufacturer of chairs and stools.

Classify the following costs by their behaviour by putting a tick in the relevant column of the table below:

Cost	Fixed	Variable	Semi-variable
• Wood used in production.			
• Advertising manager's salary.			
• Electricity costs which include a standing charge.			
• Labour costs paid on a piecework basis.			

PRACTICE QUESTIONS: SECTION 1

24 STEPPED FIXED COST

Which of the following would usually be classed as a stepped fixed cost?

A   Supervisor's wages

B   Raw materials

C   Rates

D   Telephone

25 BRAETAK LTD

Classify the following costs by their behaviour by putting a tick in the relevant column of the table below:

Cost	Fixed	Variable	Semi-variable
• Rent of an office building.			
• Wages of production staff paid on an hourly basis.			
• Wages of production staff paid by a piece rate method.			
• Sales staff paid a basic wage plus commission for each unit sold.			

26 ODO LTD

Odo Ltd is a manufacturer of clothes.

Classify the following costs by their behaviour by putting a tick in the relevant column of the table below:

Cost	Fixed	Variable	Semi-variable
• Material used in the production process.			
• Safety review fee for the year.			
• Electricity costs which include a standing charge.			
• Labour costs paid on a per unit basis.			

27 DEFINITIONS

Identify the following costs by their behaviour by putting a tick in the relevant column of the table below:

Behaviour	Fixed	Variable	Semi-variable	Stepped cost
• This type of cost increases in direct proportion to the amount of units produced.				
• This type of cost has a fixed and a variable element.				
• This type of cost remains constant despite changes in output.				
• This type of cost is fixed within a certain range of output.				

28 MATCH A GRAPH

Match a graph to each of the following costs by labelling each graph with a letter (A–E):

(a) Variable cost per unit

(b) Total fixed cost

(c) Stepped fixed costs

(d) Total variable cost

(e) Semi-variable cost

Note: Each graph may relate to more than one cost.

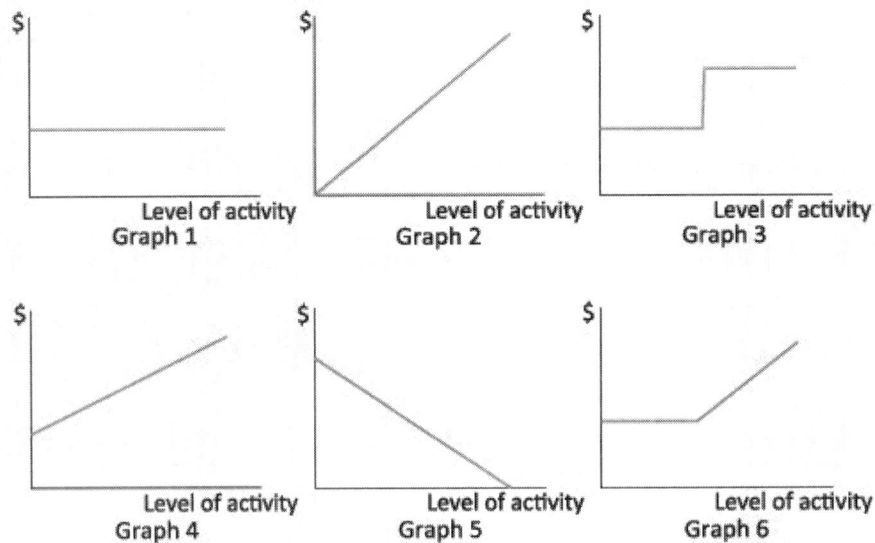

PRACTICE QUESTIONS: SECTION 1

COST CODING

29 BYTES LTD

Bytes Limited operates an IT consultancy business and uses a coding system for its elements of cost (materials, labour or overheads) and then further classifies each element by nature (direct or indirect cost) as below:

So, for example, the code for direct materials is A100.

Element of cost	Code	Nature of cost	Code
Materials	A	Direct	100
		Indirect	200
Labour	B	Direct	100
		Indirect	200
Overheads	C	Direct	100
		Indirect	200

Code the following costs, extracted from invoices and payroll, using the table below:

Cost	Code
• Salary of trainee IT consultant.	
• Planning costs to renew lease of the office.	
• Wages of the office manager.	
• Cleaning materials used by cleaner.	

30 HERO LTD

Hero Ltd, a manufacturer of superhero costumes, uses a numerical coding structure based on one profit centre and three cost centres as outlined below. Each code has a sub-code so each transaction will be coded as ***/***

Profit/cost centre	Code	Sub-classification	Sub-code
Sales	115	Women's costumes	085
		Men's costumes	095
Production	225	Direct cost	110
		Indirect cost	115
Administration	485	Direct cost	220
		Indirect cost	230
Selling and distribution	760	Direct cost	320
		Indirect cost	340

KAPLAN PUBLISHING 11

Code the following revenue and expense transactions, which have been extracted from purchase invoices, sales invoices and payroll, using the table below:

Transaction	Code
• Cost of major advertising campaign. • Oil for machinery in factory. • Silk used in manufacturing of costumes. • Insurance of head office. • Sale of women's costumes to a supermarket chain. • Wages paid to delivery van drivers.	

31 VILLAIN LTD

Villain Ltd, a mining company, uses a numerical coding structure based on one profit centre and three cost centres as outlined below. Each code has a sub-code so each transaction will be coded as ***/***

Profit/cost centre	Code	Sub-classification	Sub-code
Revenue	011	Gold sales	100
		Other sales	200
Production	015	Direct Cost	100
		Indirect Cost	200
Administration	019	Direct Cost	100
		Indirect Cost	200
Selling and distribution	024	Direct Cost	100
		Indirect Cost	200

Code the following revenue and expense transactions, which have been extracted from purchase invoices, sales invoices and payroll, using the table below:

Transaction	Code
• Petrol used to run drilling machinery. • Sale of silver to a jewellery manufacturer. • Replacement of worn out drilling machinery parts. • Depreciation of fleet of delivery lorries. • Salary of finance director. • Sale of gold to an electronics company.	

PRACTICE QUESTIONS: SECTION 1

32 NAYULZ LTD

Nayulz Limited operates a chain of nail salons across Europe and America.

Code the following transactions for the project, using the table below. Each transaction should have a five-character code.

Activity	Code	Nature of cost	Sub-code
Investments	IN	External	100
		Internal	110
Revenues	RE	Europe	225
		America	228
Costs	CO	Material	315
		Labour	318
		Overheads	325

Code the following costs, extracted from invoices and payroll, using the table below:

Cost	Code
• Income earned from salons in New York City, America.	
• Bank loans raised to open a new store in London.	
• Nail polish purchased for use in salon.	
• Heat and light for salon.	
• Nayulz funds invested in new project.	

33 JUMPER LTD

Jumper Ltd manufactures a range of different items of clothing, which it sells to various types of organisation.

The company analyses sales using an alphanumeric coding system depending on the type of clothing being sold, as well as the type of organisation the clothes are being sold to.

Type of clothing	Code
Trousers	TRS
Jumpers	KNI
Coats	MCN

Sale made to:	Code
Individuals	315
Shops	425
Offices	515
Factories	635

For example, sale of coats to a factory would be coded as MCN/635

Code the following transactions, using the table below:

Sale	Code
• Sale of one jumper to Ms. Wool.	
• Sale of protective trousers to a factory in London.	
• Sale of large coats to an office in Birmingham.	
• Sale of three hundred trousers to a shop in Manchester.	

34 GREENFINGERS

Greenfingers Ltd runs a garden centre and uses a coding system for its transactions.

Code the following transactions, using the table below. Each transaction must have a five character code.

Element of cost	Code	Nature of cost	Code
Investments	IN	External	515
		Internal	615
Revenues	RV	Plants	770
		Other	795
Costs	CS	Material	880
		Labour	890
		Overheads	900

Code the following costs, extracted from invoices and payroll, using the table below:

Cost	Code
• Purchase of seeds used to grow plants for resale.	
• External loans for investment in new greenhouses.	
• Wages of gardeners who maintain the plants to be sold.	
• Sales of food and drink.	

COST BEHAVIOUR

CALCULATION QUESTIONS

35 HULK PLC

Identify the type of cost behaviour described in each statement by putting a tick in the relevant column of the table below:

Statement	Fixed	Variable	Semi-variable
• Costs are £37,500 when 7,500 units are made and £62,500 when 12,500 units are made.			
• Costs are £2 per unit when 7,500 units are made and £1.20 per unit when 12,500 units are made.			
• Costs are £50,000 when 7,500 units are made and £80,000 when 12,500 units are made.			

36 BANNER PLC

Identify the type of cost behaviour (fixed, variable or semi-variable) described in each statement by putting a tick in the relevant column of the table below:

Statement	Fixed	Variable	Semi-variable
• Costs are £5,000 plus £45 per unit, regardless of the number of units made.			
• Costs are £5,000 when 300 units are made and £5,000 when 600 units are made.			
• Costs are £35 per unit regardless of the number of units made.			

37 NORTON PLC

Identify the type of cost behaviour (fixed, variable or semi-variable) described in each statement by putting a tick in the relevant column of the table below:

Statement	Fixed	Variable	Semi-variable
• Costs are £50,000 in total regardless of the number of units made.			
• Costs are £50,000 in total when 2,500 units are made and £80,000 when 4,000 units are made.			
• Costs are £7 per unit when 1,000 units are made and £6 per unit when 2,000 units are made.			

38 TRIUMPH LTD

Identify the type of cost behaviour (fixed, variable or semi-variable) described in each statement by ticking the relevant boxes in the table below.

Statement	Fixed	Variable	Semi-variable
At 9,000 units this cost is £29,250, and at 12,000 units it is £39,000			
At 5,000 units this cost is £5.20 per unit, and at 8,000 units it is £3.25 per unit			
At 19,800 units, this cost is £64,500, and at 27,000 units it is £82,500			

39 YOUNGS LTD

Complete the table below by inserting all costs for the different activity levels. Enter unit costs to two decimal places. All other figures must be rounded to the nearest whole pound.

	8,000 units	10,000 units	16,000 units
Variable cost (£)		50,000	
Fixed cost (£)	30,000		
Total cost (£)			110,000
Unit cost (£)			6.88

PRACTICE QUESTIONS: **SECTION 1**

40 CARE PLC

Complete the table below by inserting all costs for the different activity levels. Enter unit costs to two decimal places. All other figures must be rounded to the nearest whole pound.

	3,000 units	9,000 units	12,000 units
Variable cost (£)		37,800	
Fixed cost (£)		12,000	
Total cost (£)		49,800	
Unit cost (£)		5.53	

41 ROBSHAW LTD

Complete the table below by inserting all costs for the different activity levels. Enter unit costs to two decimal places. All other figures must be rounded to the nearest whole pound.

	9,000 units	11,000 units	16,500 units
Variable cost (£)	22,500		
Fixed cost (£)	35,000		
Total cost (£)	57,500		
Unit cost (£)	6.39		

NARRATIVE STYLE QUESTIONS

42 BUNGLE LTD

Bungle Ltd usually produces 9,000 units but is planning to increase production to 14,000 units during the next period.

Identify the following statements as either true or false by putting a tick in the relevant column of the table below:

Statement	True	False
• Total variable costs will decrease.		
• Total fixed costs will remain the same.		
• The variable cost per unit will remain the same.		
• The fixed cost per unit will increase.		

KAPLAN PUBLISHING

43 TF

Identify the following statements as either true or false by putting a tick in the relevant column of the table below:

Statement	True	False
• Variable costs change directly with changes in activity.		
• Fixed costs change directly with changes in activity.		
• Stepped costs are fixed within a set range of output.		

44 FIXED OR VARIABLE

Identify the following costs as either fixed or variable by putting a tick in the relevant column of the table below:

Cost	Fixed	Variable
• Direct materials.		
• Power used in production machinery.		
• Training costs for new employees in production.		
• Insurance for sales cars.		
• Insurance for machinery.		
• Sales commission.		

45 FOV

Identify the following costs as either fixed or variable by putting a tick in the relevant column of the table below:

Cost	Fixed	Variable
• Piecework wages paid to factory workers.		
• Salaries paid to company directors.		
• Annual payment for cleaning of air conditioning units.		

46 VOF

VOF is a company that prints magazines and newspapers.

Identify the following costs as either fixed or variable by putting a tick in the relevant column of the table below:

Cost	Fixed	Variable
• Annual salaries paid to factory managers.		
• Hourly wages paid to factory workers.		
• Colour ink used to print magazines.		

47 STORM

Indicate whether each of the following costs is an overhead or not by putting a tick in the relevant column of the table below:

Cost	Overhead?	
	Yes	No
• Labour cost of workers who assemble the product.		
• Insurance cost of factory where product is assembled.		
• Electricity for machinery.		

48 ROGUE

Indicate whether each of the following costs is an overhead or not by putting a tick in the relevant column of the table below:

Cost	Overhead?	
	Yes	No
• Labour cost of cleaning staff in a factory.		
• Depreciation of delivery vans.		
• Cost of materials used to build the product.		

49 GAMBIT

Indicate whether each of the following costs is an overhead or not by putting a tick in the relevant column of the table below:

Cost	Overhead?	
	Yes	No
• Wages of staff paid on a piecework system.		
• Cost of factory canteen staff hourly wages.		
• Direct materials.		

COST CARDS, TOTAL COSTS AND UNIT COSTS

50 JEEPERS LTD

Indicate whether the following costs are direct or not by putting a tick in the relevant column of the table below:

Cost	Direct	Indirect
• Materials used in production.		
• Piecework labour costs.		
• Salary of chief executive.		

Jeepers Ltd makes a single product. At a production level of 15,000 units, the company has the following costs:

Materials   37,500 kilos at £14.00 per kilo

Labour   7,500 hours at £16.00 per hour

Overheads   £570,000

Complete the table below to show the unit product cost at the production level of 15,000 units. Overheads are absorbed on a cost per unit basis. Enter your answer to the nearest pound.

Element	Unit product cost £
Materials	
Labour	
Direct cost	
Overheads	
Total	

51 BRANIAC LTD

Braniac Ltd makes a single product. A production level of 55,000 units has the following costs:

Materials   96,250 litres at £14 per litre

Labour   192,500 hours at £11.50 per hour

Overheads   £687,500

Complete the table below to show the total cost per unit at a production level of 55,000 units, absorbing overheads on a per unit basis. Enter your answers to two decimal places.

Element	Unit cost
Materials	
Labour	
Direct cost	
Overheads	
Total	

52 MARKO LTD

Marko Ltd is costing a single product which has the following cost details:

Variable costs per unit
Materials £2
Labour £3
Royalties £0.50

Total fixed costs
Production overhead £80,000
Sales and distribution £90,000

Complete the following total cost and unit cost table for a production level of 20,000 units. Give your answer to the nearest penny for the unit cost and the nearest pound for the total cost.

	Unit cost	Total cost for 20,000 units
Variable production costs		
Fixed production costs		
Total production cost		

53 BIZARRO LTD

Bizarro Ltd makes a single product and for a production level of 17,000 units has the following cost details:

	Per unit	Cost
Materials	2.5kg	£18/kilo
Labour	1.0hrs	£9/hour
Fixed overheads		£42,500

Complete the table below to show the unit cost and total cost at the production level of 17,000 units. Overheads are absorbed on a cost per unit basis. Give your answer to the nearest penny for the unit cost and the nearest pound for total cost.

Element	Unit cost	Total cost
Materials		
Labour		
Overheads		
Total		

54 VINNY LTD

Vinny Ltd is a commercial laundrette below are the costings for 15,000 units:

Variable costs
Materials   £75,000
Labour   £120,000
Fixed costs
Production overhead   £100,000

Complete the table below to show the total cost and total cost per unit at a production level of 15,000 units, absorbing overheads on a per unit basis. Enter your answers to two decimal places for the unit cost and the nearest whole pound for total cost.

	Unit cost	Total cost
PICKLIST	£5	£75,000
Labour	£8.00	£120,000
Direct costs	£13.00	£195,000
PICKLIST	£6.67	£100,000
Total cost	£19.67	£295,000

Options for picklists:

Materials
WIP
Finished goods
Overheads

55 DARKSEID LTD

Darkseid Ltd makes a single product and for a production level of 95,000 units has the following cost details:

Materials	47,500kg	at £7/kilo
Labour	71,250hrs	at £9/hour
Fixed overheads		£242,000

Complete the table below to show the unit cost at a REVISED production level of 100,000 units. Overheads are absorbed on a cost per unit basis. Give your answer to the nearest penny.

Element	Unit cost
Materials	£3.50
Labour	£6.75
Fixed overheads	£2.42
Total	£12.67

56 OLSEN LTD

Olsen Ltd is costing a single product which has the following cost details:

Variable costs	Per unit
Materials	£12
Labour	£17

Total Fixed Costs

Production overhead   £80,000
Administration overhead   £40,000

Complete the table below to show the total cost per unit at a production level of 80,000 units, absorbing overheads on a per unit basis. Enter your answers to two decimal places for the unit cost.

Element	Unit cost
Materials	
Labour	
Direct cost	
Production overheads	
Total cost per unit	

57 FLAKEWAY LTD

Flakeway Ltd makes a single product and for a production level of 24,000 units has the following cost details:

Materials	6,000kg	at £20/kilo
Labour	8,000hrs	at £12/hour
Fixed overheads		£48,000

Complete the table below to show the unit cost at the production level of 24,000 units. Overheads are absorbed on a cost per unit basis. Enter your answers to two decimal places.

Element	Unit cost
PICKLIST	£5
Labour	
PICKLIST	£9
PICKLIST	
Total	

Options for picklists:

Materials
Direct cost
Labour
Finished goods
Overheads

58 CORONATION LTD

Coronation Ltd is costing a single product which has the following cost details

Variable costs	Per unit	Cost
Materials	50g	£10/kg
Labour	1hr	£6/hour

Total fixed costs

Production overhead   £40,000
Administration overhead   £20,000
Sales and distribution   £25,000

Complete the following total cost and unit cost table for a production level of 5,000 units. Overheads are absorbed on a cost per unit basis. Give your answer to the nearest penny for the unit cost and the nearest pound for total cost.

	Total cost for 5,000 units
Direct costs	
Production overhead	
Non production overhead	
Total costs	

59 LUTHOR LTD

Luthor Ltd makes a single product and for a production level of 15,000 units has the following cost details:

Materials	60,000kg	at £15/kilo
Labour	37,500hrs	at £9/hour
Fixed overheads		£570,000

Complete the table below to show the unit cost at the production level of 15,000 units. Overheads are absorbed on a cost per unit basis. Give your answer to the nearest penny.

Element	Unit cost
Materials	
Labour	
Fixed overheads	
Total	

OVERHEAD ABSORPTION

60 WILKINSON LTD

Wilkinson Ltd is looking to calculate the unit cost for one of the products it makes. It needs to calculate an overhead absorption rate to apply to each unit.

Total factory activity is forecast as follows:

Machine hours	10,000
Labour hours	12,500
Units	60,000
Overheads	£150,000

(a) Complete the table below to show the possible overhead absorption rates that Wilkinson Ltd could use. Enter values two decimal places.

	Machine hour	Labour hour	Unit
Overheads (£)			
Activity			
Absorption rate (£)			

The following data relates to making one unit of the product:

Material	2 kilos at £5 per kilo
Labour	15 minutes at £10 per hour
Production time	10 minutes

(b) Complete the table below to calculate the total unit cost, using the three overhead absorption rates you have calculated in part (a). Enter values to two decimal places.

Cost	Machine hour (£)	Labour hour (£)	Unit (£)
Material			
Labour			
Direct cost			
Overheads			
Total unit cost			

61 HODGSON LTD

Hodgson Ltd is looking to calculate the unit cost for one of the products it makes. It needs to calculate an overhead absorption rate to apply to each unit.

Total factory activity is forecast as follows:

Machine hours	15,000
Labour hours	20,000
Units	100,000
Overheads	£250,000

(a) Complete the table below to show the possible overhead absorption rates that Hodgson Ltd could use. Enter values to two decimal places.

	Machine hour	Labour hour	Unit
Overheads (£)			
Activity			
Absorption rate (£)			

The following data relates to making one unit of the product:

Material	4 kilos at £6 per kilo
Labour	30 minutes at £12 per hour
Production time	20 minutes

(b) Complete the table below to calculate the total unit cost, using the three overhead absorption rates you have calculated in part a. Enter values to two decimal places.

Cost	Machine hour (£)	Labour hour (£)	Unit (£)
Material			
Labour			
Direct cost			
Overheads			
Total unit cost			

62 BARNES LTD

Barnes Ltd is looking to calculate the unit cost for one of the products it makes. It needs to calculate an overhead absorption rate to apply to each unit.

Total factory activity is forecast as follows:

Machine hours	17,500
Labour hours	12,000
Units	40,000
Overheads	£130,000

Complete the table below to show what the overhead cost per unit would be using the three possible absorption methods. Enter the absorption rates to two decimal places.

	Machine hour	Labour hour	Unit
No. hours/units			
Hours per unit			
Absorption rate (£)			
Overhead per unit (£)			

63 MAJA LTD

Maja Ltd is looking to calculate the unit cost for one of the products it makes. It needs to calculate an overhead absorption rate to apply to each unit.

Total factory activity is forecast as follows:

Machine hours	9,000
Labour hours	11,000
Units	60,000
Overheads	£145,000

Complete the table below to show what the overhead cost per unit would be using the three possible absorption methods.

	Machine hour	Labour hour	Unit
No. hours/units			
Hours per unit			
Absorption rate (£)			
Overhead per unit (£)			

AAT: PRINCIPLES OF COSTING

MANUFACTURING ACCOUNTS

64 JOKER LTD

Reorder the following costs into a manufacturing account format on the right side of the table below for the year ended 31 December.

	£		£
Closing inventory of work in progress	52,000		
Direct labour	140,000		
Opening inventory of raw materials	50,000		
Closing inventory of finished goods	61,000		
Closing inventory of raw materials	65,000		
Manufacturing overheads	85,000		
COST OF GOODS SOLD			
MANUFACTURING COST			
Purchases of raw materials	120,000		
Opening inventory of work in progress	48,000		
Opening inventory of finished goods	57,000		
DIRECT COST			
DIRECT MATERIALS USED			
COST OF GOODS MANUFACTURED			

Enter the correct figures for the following costs which were not provided in the table above.

	£
DIRECT MATERIALS USED	
DIRECT COST	
MANUFACTURING COST	
COST OF GOODS MANUFACTURED	
COST OF GOODS SOLD	

65 TUT LTD

Complete the following manufacturing account by selecting from the drop-down picklist and entering values in the blank cells.

	£
Opening inventory of raw materials	10,000
Purchases of raw materials	60,000
Closing inventory of raw materials	12,000
PICKLIST	
Direct labour	88,000
PICKLIST	
Manufacturing overheads	45,000
PICKLIST	
Opening inventory of work in progress	12,000
Closing inventory of work in progress	15,000
PICKLIST	
Opening inventory of finished goods	18,000
Closing inventory of finished goods	20,000
PICKLIST	

Options for picklist:

| COST OF GOODS MANUFACTURED |
| DIRECT MATERIALS USED |
| COST OF GOODS SOLD |
| MANUFACTURING COST |
| DIRECT COST |

66 RIDDLER LTD

Riddler Ltd has the following cost information for its last quarter:

	£
Materials costs:	
Materials forming part of the product	100,000
Materials not forming part of the product	25,000
Labour costs:	
Labour working on production	194,000
Labour supporting work on production	12,000
Factory indirect expenses	75,000

Relevant inventory changes were as follows:

	£
Raw materials:	
Opening	20,000
Closing	22,000
Work in progress:	
Opening	31,000
Closing	35,000
Finished goods:	
Opening	60,000
Closing	50,000

Complete the table below to show Riddler's cost structure for the last quarter:

	£
Direct cost	
Manufacturing overhead	
Total manufacturing cost	
Cost of goods manufactured	
Cost of goods sold	

67 CLOCKING LTD

Clocking Ltd has the following information for its last quarter:

	£
Materials costs:	
Direct	50,000
Indirect	8,000
Labour costs:	
Direct	97,000
Indirect	10,000
Factory indirect expenses	53,000

Relevant inventory changes were as follows:

	£
Raw materials:	
Opening	7,000
Closing	10,000
Work in progress:	
Opening	8,000
Closing	10,000
Finished goods:	
Opening	30,000
Closing	25,000

Complete the table below to show Clocking Ltd's cost structure for the last quarter:

	£
Direct cost	
Manufacturing overhead	
Total manufacturing cost	
Cost of goods manufactured	
Cost of goods sold	

68 BOOKWORM LTD

The below information relates to the manufacturing costs of Bookworm's sole product.

	£
Direct labour	15,000
Opening inventory of raw materials	5,000
Closing inventory of finished goods	16,000
Purchases of raw materials	15,000
Manufacturing overheads	25,000
Closing inventory of raw materials	8,000
Opening inventory of finished goods	12,000
Opening inventory of work in progress	4,000
Closing inventory of work in progress	6,000

Complete the table below to show the values for inclusion within Bookworm's manufacturing account.

	£
Direct materials used	12,000
Direct cost	27,000
Manufacturing cost	52,000
Cost of goods manufactured	50,000
Cost of goods sold	46,000

69 MULTI

Within a manufacturing account, the manufacturing costs are £45,000. Opening work in progress is £11,000, while opening finished goods were costed at £8,100. Closing work in progress is £9,700, while closing finished goods were £8,900.

What is Multi's cost of goods sold?

A £44,500

B £48,700

C £45,500

D £41,300

PRACTICE QUESTIONS: SECTION 1

COSTING FOR INVENTORY AND WORK-IN-PROGRESS

NARRATIVE STYLE QUESTIONS

70 BOBBLE LTD

Match the disadvantage to the method of stock valuation.

Characteristic	
• Potentially out of date valuation on issues.	
• The valuation of inventory rarely reflects the actual purchase price of the material.	
• Potentially out of date closing inventory valuation.	

Options:

FIFO
LIFO
AVCO

71 LINT LTD

Identify the following statements as either true or false by putting a tick in the relevant column of the table below:

Statement	True	False
• In periods of rising prices, FIFO gives a higher valuation of closing inventory than LIFO or AVCO.		
• In periods of falling prices, LIFO gives a higher valuation of issues of inventory than FIFO or AVCO.		
• AVCO would normally be expected to produce a valuation of closing inventory somewhere between valuations under FIFO and LIFO.		

72 FLUFF LTD

Identify the correct inventory valuation method from the characteristic given by putting a tick in the relevant column of the table below:

Characteristic	FIFO	LIFO	AVCO
• This inventory valuation method is particularly suited to inventory that consist of liquid materials e.g. oil.			
• This inventory valuation method is particularly suited to inventory that has a short shelf life e.g. dairy products.			
• This inventory valuation method is suited to a wheat farmer who has large silos of grain. Grain is added to and taken from the top of these silos.			

73 FIDO LTD

Identify the correct inventory valuation method from the characteristic given by putting a tick in the relevant column of the table below:

Characteristic	FIFO	LIFO	AVCO
• In times of rising prices this method will give higher profits.			
• In times of rising prices this method will give lower profits.			
• In times of rising prices this method gives a middle level of profits compared to the other two.			

74 TRUFFEAUX LTD

Identify whether the following statements are true or false by putting a tick in the relevant column of the table below:

Statement	True	False
• FIFO costs issues of inventory at the most recent purchase price.		
• AVCO costs issues of inventory at the oldest purchase price.		
• LIFO costs issues of inventory at the oldest purchase price.		
• FIFO values closing inventory at the most recent purchase price.		
• LIFO values closing inventory at the most recent purchase price.		
• AVCO values closing inventory at the latest purchase price.		

75 STOCKY LTD

Identify the correct inventory valuation method from the characteristic given by putting a tick in the relevant column of the table below:

Characteristic	FIFO	LIFO	AVCO
• Issues are valued at the most recent purchase cost.			
• Inventory is valued at the average of the cost of purchases.			
• Inventory is valued at the most recent purchase cost.			

76 BUFFER

A company is considering its inventory control policy. At present it does not hold any buffer inventory. Identify whether the following changes would be likely to arise as a result of introducing buffer inventory.

	TRUE	FALSE
• Holding costs per unit of inventory would increase		
• Average inventory levels would reduce		

77 INVENTORY

A company prefers to hold a high level of buffer inventory. It has discovered that the rental cost for the storage space that it uses to hold the buffer inventory will increase next year. Identify whether the following statements are true or false if the company maintains its high inventory levels.

	TRUE	FALSE
• Inventory levels will increase		
• Inventory holding costs will increase		

IDENTIFICATION OF INVENTORY VALUATION METHOD

78 EPIC LTD

You are told that the opening inventory of a single raw material in the stores is 8,000 units at £5 per unit. During the month, 12,000 units at £4.50 were received and the following week 14,000 units were issued.

(a) **Identify the valuation method described in the statements below**

Characteristic	
• Closing inventory is valued at £28,200. • The issue of inventory is valued at £67,000. • The issue of inventory is valued at £64,000.	

Options:

FIFO
LIFO
AVCO

(b) **Identify whether the statements in the table below are true or false by putting a tick in the relevant column.**

	True	False
• AVCO values the issue of inventory at £65,800.		
• LIFO values the closing inventory at £27,000.		
• FIFO values the closing inventory at £30,000.		

79 AWESOME LTD

You are told that the opening inventory of a single raw material in the stores is 6,000 units at £6 per unit. During the month, another 6,000 units at £10 were received and the following week 7,150 units were issued.

(a) Identify the valuation method described in the statements below:

Characteristic	
• Closing inventory is valued at £48,500.	
• The issue of inventory is valued at £57,200.	
• The issue of inventory is valued at £66,900.	

Options:

FIFO
LIFO
AVCO

(b) Identify whether the statements in the table below are true or false by putting a tick in the relevant column.

	True	False
• FIFO values the issue of inventory at £47,500.		
• AVCO values the closing inventory at £38,400.		
• LIFO values the closing inventory at £29,100.		

80 AMAZING LTD

You are told that the opening inventory of a single raw material in the stores is 2,000 units at £1.50 per unit. During the month, another 5,000 units at £5 were received and the following week 6,000 units were issued.

(a) Identify the valuation method described in the statements below:

Characteristic	FIFO	LIFO	AVCO
• Closing inventory is valued at £1,500.			
• The issue of inventory is valued at £23,000.			
• The issue of inventory is valued at £24,000.			

(b) Identify whether the statements in the table below are true or false by putting a tick in the relevant column.

	True	False
• LIFO values the issue of inventory at £26,500.		
• AVCO values the closing inventory at £5,000.		
• LIFO values the closing inventory at £4,000.		

INVENTORY CARDS

81 STONE LTD

Stone Ltd sells stone to builders. It had the following movements in one type of stone for the month of June.

DATE	RECEIPTS		ISSUES	
	Tonnes	Cost	Tonnes	Cost
June 1	500	£7,500		
June 8	350	£6,125		
June 15	275	£4,950		
June 22			650	
June 29	500	£8,750		

Complete the table below for the issue and closing inventory values, stating your answers to the nearest pound.

Method	Cost of issue on 22 June	Closing inventory at 30 June
FIFO		
LIFO		
AVCO		

82 NATAL LTD

Natal Ltd makes and sells a wide range of clothes for babies. The following is an inventory card for Natal's most popular product for the month of December.

DATE	RECEIPTS		ISSUES	
	Units	Cost	Units	Cost
December 3	10,000	£85,000		
December 18	14,000	£112,000		
December 19	50,000	£350,000		
December 25			72,500	
December 29	5,000	£30,000		

(a) Complete the table below for the issue and closing inventory values. Give your answers to the nearest pound.

Method	Cost of issue on 25 Dec	Closing inventory at 29 Dec
LIFO		
AVCO		

(b) Identify the following statements as true or false by putting a tick in the relevant column of the table below:

	True	False
• FIFO would give a lower closing inventory valuation on the 29 December than LIFO and AVCO.		
• FIFO would give a lower cost of issue on the 25 December than LIFO and AVCO.		

83 GANDALF LTD

Gandalf Ltd has the following movements in a certain type of inventory into and out of its stores for the month of July.

DATE	RECEIPTS			ISSUES			BALANCE
	Units	Unit cost	Total £	Units	Unit cost	Total £	Total £
July 2	600	£1.50	£900				
July 4	500	£1.70	£850				
July 15				620			
July 19	200	£1.80	£360				
July 31				400			

Calculate the costs of the issues made on July 15 and July 31 if Gandalf plc uses a LIFO inventory valuation method.

	Valuation £
• July 15	
• July 31	

84 GRUNDY LTD

Grundy Ltd has the following movements in a certain type of inventory into and out of its stores for the month of October.

DATE	RECEIPTS		ISSUES	
	Units	Cost	Units	Cost
October 9	6000	£15,000		
October 12	3000	£6,000		
October 20	3000	£3,000		
October 25			8500	
October 30	1000	£1,500		

Complete the table below for the issue and closing inventory values.

Method	Cost of issue on 25 October	Closing inventory at 31 October
FIFO		
LIFO		
AVCO		

85 LOBO LTD

Lobo Ltd has the following movements in a certain type of inventory into and out of its stores for the month of May.

DATE	RECEIPTS		ISSUES	
	Units	Cost	Units	Cost
May 12	250	£1,375		
May 17	400	£1,800		
May 18	600	£1,200		
May 29			500	
May 30	100	£375		

Complete the table below for the issue and closing inventory values.

Method	Cost of issue on 29 May	Closing inventory at 30 May
FIFO		
LIFO		
AVCO		

86 ZOD LTD

Zod Ltd has the following movements in a certain type of inventory into and out of it stores for the month of February.

DATE	RECEIPTS		ISSUES	
	Units	Cost	Units	Cost
February 2	100	£500		
February 3			50	
February 12	150	£600		
February 16			60	
February 20	110	£505		
February 26			40	

Complete the table below for the issue and closing inventory values. State your answer to the nearest pound.

Method	Cost of issue on 16 February	Closing inventory at 26 February
FIFO		
AVCO		

PRACTICE QUESTIONS: SECTION 1

COSTING FOR LABOUR

NARRATIVE STYLE QUESTIONS

87 NULAB LTD

Identify the labour payment method by putting a tick in the relevant column of the table below:

Payment method	Time-rate	Piecework	Piece-rate plus bonus
• Labour is paid based solely on the production achieved.			
• Labour is paid extra if an agreed level of output is exceeded.			
• Labour is paid according to hours worked.			

88 LU LTD

Identify one advantage for each labour payment method by putting a tick in the relevant column of the table below:

Payment method	Time-rate	Piecework	Time-rate plus bonus
• Assured level of remuneration for employee.			
• Employee earns more if they work more efficiently than expected.			
• Assured level of remuneration and reward for working efficiently.			

89 MANDELA LTD

Identify whether the following statements are true or false in the relevant column of the table below:

Statement	True	False
• Time rate is paid based on the production achieved.		
• Overtime is paid for hours worked over the standard hours agreed.		
• Piece rate is paid according to hours worked.		

90 PERRES LTD

Identify the hourly payment method by choosing from the options.

Payment method	
• This is the amount paid above the basic rate for hours worked in excess of the normal hours.	
• This is the total amount paid per hour for hours worked in excess of the normal hours.	
• This is the amount paid per hour for normal hours worked.	

Options:

Basic rate
Overtime premium
Overtime rate

91 TEVEZ LTD

Identify the following statements as true or false by putting a tick in the relevant column of the table below:

Statement	True	False
• Direct labour costs can be identified with the goods being made or the service being provided.		
• Indirect labour costs vary directly with the level of activity.		

92 BERDYCH LTD

Identify the whether the labour payment is usually associated with a fixed or variable cost by putting a tick in the relevant column of the table below:

Payment method	Variable	Fixed
• Labour that is paid based on a time rate basis per hour worked.		
• Labour is paid on a monthly salary basis.		
• Labour that is based on number of units produced.		

PRACTICE QUESTIONS: SECTION 1

93 SODERLING LTD

Identify each labour payment method by choosing from the options.

Payment method	
• Assured level of remuneration for employee usually agreed for the year. • Employee earnings are directly linked with units they produce. • Employee earnings are directly linked with hours they work.	

Options:

Time-rate
Piecework
Salary

94 MURRAY LTD

Identify the following statements as true or false by putting a tick in the relevant column of the table below:

	True	False
• Indirect labour costs includes production supervisors' salaries.		
• Direct labour costs usually vary directly with the level of activity.		

95 OLGA LTD

Identify one advantage for each labour payment method by putting a tick in the relevant column of the table below:

Payment method	Time-rate	Piecework	Salary
• Employee is paid the same amount every month.			
• Employee wage increases in direct correlation with the number of hours worked.			
• Employee wage increases in direct correlation with the number of units produced.			

96 PIECEWORK STATEMENTS

Identify the following statements as either true or false by putting a tick in the relevant column of the table below:

Statement	True	False
• Piecework encourages employees to work harder.		
• Piecework requires accurate recording of the number of hours staff have worked.		
• Piecework encourages workers to improve the quality of the units they produce.		

CALCULATING LABOUR COSTS

97 MUTANT LTD

Mutant Ltd pays a time-rate of £7.50 per hour to its direct labour for a standard 32 hour week. Any of the labour force working in excess of 32 hours is paid an overtime rate of time and a half.

Calculate the following figures for the week for the two workers in the table below, entering your answers to the nearest pound.

Worker	Hours worked	Basic wage	Overtime	Gross wage
S. Torm	34 hours			
J. Grey	38 hours			

98 PHOENIX LTD

Phoenix plc pays its employees £8.00 per hour and expects them to make 20 units per hour. Any excess production will be paid a bonus of £1.50 per unit.

Identify the following statements as being true or false by putting a tick in the relevant column of the table below:

Statement	True	False
An employee who works 38 hours and makes 775 units will not receive a bonus.		
An employee who works 40 hours and makes 815 units will receive total pay of £342.50.		
An employee who works 37 hours and makes 744 units will earn a bonus of £6.		

99 KAHN LTD

Kahn Ltd uses a time-rate method with bonus to pay its direct labour in one of its factories. The time-rate used is £12 per hour and a worker is expected to produce 5 units an hour, any time saved is paid at £6 per hour.

Calculate the gross wage for the week including bonus for the three workers in the table below:

Worker	Hours worked	Units produced	Basic wage	Bonus	Gross wage
A. Smith	35	175			
J. O'Hara	35	180			
M. Stizgt	35	185			

100 ENTERPRISE LTD

Enterprise Ltd has a production target for its employees of 400 units per week. Employees are rewarded with a bonus for excess production, at a rate of £6 per unit, capped at a maximum of 450 units.

Identify whether the bonus calculations for the following employees are correct:

Bonus calculation	Correct	Incorrect
Javier produced 400 units and earned a bonus of £6.		
Esha produced 465 units and earned a bonus of £390.		
Mika produced 480 units and earned a bonus of £300.		

101 SGC LTD

SGC Ltd uses a basic salary plus piecework method to pay labour in one of its factories. The basic salary is £285 per week the piece rate used is £0.75 per unit produced.

Calculate the gross wage for the week for the two workers in the table below. Enter your answer to the nearest penny.

Worker	Units produced in week	Gross wage
J. O'Neill	500 units	
S. Carter	650 units	

102 GOTHIC LTD

Gothic Ltd employs 5 production workers in its factory. All production workers are paid a basic rate of £17 per hour.

The factory sets a total production target for output each week, at 20,000 units. A bonus of £30 per worker is paid for each complete percent that actual output exceeds the target.

Last week, the actual output was 22,100 units.

Identify whether the following statements about the labour cost for Gothic Ltd are correct or incorrect for the following employees:

Pay calculation	Correct	Incorrect
M. Shelley worked for 35 hours and earned total income of £595.		
G. Leroux worked for 37 hours and earned total income of £929.		
A.E. Poe worked for 32 hours and earned total income of £874.		
The total bonus paid by Gothic Ltd was £1,500.		

103 AVENGERS LTD

Avengers Ltd pays a time-rate of £10 per hour to its direct labour force a standard 35 hour week. Any of the labour force working in excess of this over the four week period is paid an overtime rate of time and a quarter.

Calculate the gross wage for the **4-week** period for the three workers in the table below. Enter your answers to the nearest pound.

Worker	Hours worked	Basic wage	Overtime	Gross wage
T. Stark	138			
B. Banner	142			
S. Rogers	145			

104 DRACO LTD

Draco Ltd uses a piecework method to pay labour in one of its factories. The rate used is 80p per unit produced up to the standard number of units to be produced per week of 250. For any units over that the workers will get £10 per 20 units.

Calculate the gross wage for the week for the three workers in the table below:

Worker	Units produced in week	Gross wage
P. Jones	240 units	
D. Bannatyne	350 units	
L. Redford	250 units	

105 QUAGGA PLC

Quagga plc pays its employees £4.50 per hour and expects them to make 50 units per hour. Any excess production will be paid a bonus of 45p per unit.

Identify the following statements as being true or false by putting a tick in the relevant column of the table below:

Statement	True	False
During a 29 hour week, an employee producing 1,475 units would not receive a bonus.		✓
During a 32 hour week, an employee producing 1,665 units would receive a bonus of £29.25.	✓	
During a 37 hour week, an employee producing 1,925 units would receive total pay of £300.25.		✓

106 JLA PLC

JLA plc pays its employees £5 per hour and expects them to make 6 units per hour. Any time saved will be paid as a bonus at £8 per hour.

Identify the following statements as being true or false by putting a tick in the relevant column of the table below:

Statement	True	False
During a 30 hour week, an employee producing 192 units would receive a bonus of £16.		✓
During a 35 hour week, an employee producing 240 units would receive total pay of £215.	✓	
During a 30 hour week, an employee producing 180 units would not receive a bonus.	✓	

107 INJUSTICE LTD

Davidson Ltd pays a basic wage of £175/week plus £1.20 per unit produced.

Calculate the gross wage for the week for the three workers in the table below:

Worker	Units produced	Basic wage	Piece work	Gross wage
N. Wing	295	£175	£354.00	£529.00
W. Woman	355	£175	£426.00	£601.00
T. Flash	385	£175	£462.00	£637.00

108 GREENWOOD LTD

Greenwood Ltd pays a basic wage of £350/week equivalent to a time-rate of £10 per hour and a standard 35 hour week. Workers are expected to produce 5 units an hour and for units produced in excess of this a bonus is paid based on £7 for every hour saved.

So, for example, if 10 additional units are produced, then this would be equivalent to two hours saved and a bonus of £14 awarded.

Calculate the gross wage for the week including bonus for the three workers in the table below:

Worker	Hours worked	Units produced	Basic wage	Bonus	Gross wage
B. Ryan	35	175			
S. Chang	35	190			
E. Schneider	35	210			

109 SANCHO LTD

Sancho Ltd pays a time-rate of £18 per hour for a standard 35 hour week. The basic wage for 35 hours is guaranteed but no overtime is paid for additional hours beyond this standard 35 hours.

However teams of three staff are given a target of producing 300 units in total for the team across the week. Any extra units above this target entitle all members of the team to a bonus of £20 per extra unit produced.

The workers in the following table work in a single team. Calculate the gross wage for the week including bonus for the three workers in the table below:

Worker	Hours worked	Units produced	Basic wage	Bonus	Gross wage
A. Ali	38	115			
B. Jiou	33	100			
C. Perry	35	94			

PRACTICE QUESTIONS: SECTION 1

BUDGETING AND VARIANCES

NARRATIVE QUESTIONS

110 PIERRE LTD

Identify the following statements as being true or false by putting a tick in the relevant column of the table below:

Statement	True	False
Fixed budgets are prepared at the start of a budget period and are not adjusted to reflect changes during the period		
Flexible budgets can be prepared at the start of the budget period and can be adjusted to reflect changes in activity level during the period		

111 NIXON LTD

Identify the following statements as being true or false by putting a tick in the relevant column of the table below:

Statement	True	False
One of the purposes of a budget is to ensure that production levels are coordinated with expected sales levels		
One of the purposes of budgets is to ensure that staff are aware that all responsibilities are carried out by senior management		

112 VARIOUS LTD

Identify the following statements as being true or false by putting a tick in the relevant column of the table below:

Statement	True	False
• A variance is the difference between budgeted and actual cost. • A favourable variance could arise due to actual costs being less than budgeted. • An adverse variance could arise due to actual income being less than budgeted. • A favourable variance occurs when actual income is the same as budgeted income.		

KAPLAN PUBLISHING

113 NOOR LTD

Identify the following statements as being true or false by putting a tick in the relevant column of the table below:

Statement	True	False
If budgeted sales are 6,000 units at £7.50 per unit and actual sales are £47,600, the sales variance is favourable		
A favourable cost variance occurs when an actual cost of £9,800 is compared to a budgeted cost of £24 per unit for a budgeted output of 400 units		
A variance arises from a comparison of budgeted costs for last year with actual costs for this year		
If actual material costs are the same as budgeted costs for materials then no variance arises		

114 GATLAND LTD

Identify the following statements as being true or false by putting a tick in the relevant column of the table below:

Statement	True	False
If budgeted sales are 4,000 units at £9.50 per unit and actual sales are £35,200, the sales variance is favourable		
A favourable cost variance occurs when an actual cost of £6,400 is compared to a budgeted cost of £14 per unit for a budgeted output of 500 units		
A variance arises from a comparison of budgeted costs for last year with budgeted costs for this year		
If actual material costs are the same as budgeted costs for materials then the materials variance is adverse		

115 LANCASTER LTD

Identify the following statements as being true or false by putting a tick in the relevant column of the table below:

Statement	True	False
If budgeted sales are 14,000 units at £3.50 per unit and actual sales are £45,200, the sales variance is favourable		
An adverse cost variance occurs when an actual cost of £68,400 is compared to a budgeted cost of £14 per unit for a budgeted output of 5,000 units		
A variance arises from a comparison of budgeted costs for this year with actual costs for this year		
If actual material costs are the same as budgeted costs for materials then the materials variance is favourable		

116 GOODE LTD

Identify the following statements as being true or false by putting a tick in the relevant column of the table below:

Statement	True	False
The variance for the Direct Material cost of Department B should be reported to the purchasing manager		
The variance for the Direct Labour cost for Department A should be reported to the sales manager		
The variance for the Direct Labour cost for Department B should be reported to the production manager of Department A		
A Direct Material cost variance that has been deemed Not Significant should not be reported		

117 BROWN LTD

Identify the following statements as being true or false by putting a tick in the relevant column of the table below:

Statement	True	False
The variance for the Direct Material cost of Department A should be reported to the purchasing manager		
The variance for the Direct Labour cost for Department A should be reported to the production manager of Department B		
The variance for sales should be reported to the sales manager		
A Direct Material cost variance that has been deemed Significant should not be reported		

118 MAGENTA LTD

Identify the following statements as being true or false by putting a tick in the relevant column of the table below:

Statement	True	False
An increase in the production workers' hourly rate of pay could result in an adverse labour variance		
An increase in the efficiency of the production workers could result in an adverse labour variance		

119 CARLOTA LTD

Identify the following statements as being true or false by putting a tick in the relevant column of the table below:

Statement	True	False
Increasing the selling price per unit might result in a favourable sales variance		
Increased competition from rival companies might result in a favourable sales variance		

CALCULATION QUESTIONS

120 FUNKY LTD

Funky Ltd manufactures a single product which has the following cost details for its upcoming year:

Budgeted output	3,000 units	
Selling price	£90 per unit	
Direct materials	2 kg per unit	£10/kg
Direct labour	2 hours per unit	£6 per hour
Fixed overheads	£40,000	

Complete the following budget to calculate the profit or loss for the year. Enter values to the nearest whole pound.

	Budget £ 3,000 units
Sales revenue	
Direct materials	
Direct labour	
Fixed overhead	
Profit/loss	

121 EREBOR LTD

Erebor Ltd has produced a performance report detailing budgeted and actual cost for last month.

Calculate the amount of the variance for each cost type and then determine whether it is adverse or favourable (enter A or F).

Cost type	Budget £	Actual £	Variance £	Adverse or favourable (A or F)
Sales	600,500	597,800		
Direct materials	205,800	208,500		
Direct labour	155,000	154,800		
Production overheads	65,000	72,100		
Administration overheads	58,400	55,200		

122 MORIA LTD

The following performance report for this month has been produced for Moria Ltd. Any variance in excess of 7% of budget is deemed to be significant.

Calculate the variance as a % of the budget and enter your answer into the table below to the **nearest whole percentage**. Indicate whether the variance is significant or not by entering S for significant and NS for not significant.

Cost type	Budget	Variance	Variance as % of budget	Significant or Not significant
Sales	45,100	4,214		
Material	15,750	1,260		
Labour	12,915	805		
Variable overheads	5,750	315		
Fixed overheads	8,155	1,011		

123 WYEDALE LTD

Wyedale Ltd has produced a performance report detailing budgeted and actual cost for last month.

Calculate the amount of the variance in £ and % for each cost type and then determine whether it is adverse or favourable by putting an A or F in the relevant column of the table below. State your percentage to the nearest whole number.

Cost type	Budget £	Actual £	Variance £	Variance %	Adverse/ Favourable
Sales	27,000	29,775			
Direct materials	7,400	8,510			
Direct labour	7,200	7,920			
Production overheads	5,500	5,390			
Administration overheads	4,500	4,365			

PRACTICE QUESTIONS: SECTION 1

124 BELEGOST LTD

The following performance report for this month has been produced for Belegost Ltd as summarised in the table below. Any variance in excess of 6% of budget is deemed to be significant and should be reported to the relevant manager for review and appropriate action.

Determine whether the variance for each figure is adverse or favourable by putting an A or F into the relevant column of the table below. Put an S in the relevant column if the variance is significant or an NS if the variance is not significant.

	Budget £	Actual £	Adverse or Favourable (A or F)	Significant or not significant (S or NS)
Sales	205,000	207,100		
Direct materials	75,150	78,750		
Direct labour	110,556	107,950		
Production overheads	14,190	12,500		
Non-production overheads	16,190	17,880		

125 IVAN LTD

Ivan Ltd produces a single product. You have been provided with the following budget information for a production level of 20,000 units.

Selling price	£27 per unit	
Direct materials	5 kg per unit	£0.50/kg
Direct labour	0.25 hours per unit	£25 per hour
Fixed overheads	£120,000	

Complete the following table showing the budgeted figures at a production level of 20,000 units and the variance for each item. Determine whether each variance is adverse or favourable. Enter monetary values to the nearest whole pound.

	Budget £	Actual £	Variance £	Adverse or Favourable
Sales		547,450		
Direct materials		80,200		
Direct labour		146,000		
Fixed overheads		144,200		
Profit/loss		177,050		

AAT: PRINCIPLES OF COSTING

126 BLUEBELL LTD

The following performance report for this month has been produced for Bluebell Ltd as summarised in the table below.

Calculate the variances in the table below and indicate whether they are adverse or favourable by putting an A or F in the relevant column and calculate the variance as a % to the nearest whole number.

Cost type	Budget £	Actual £	Variance £	Adv/ Fav	%
Sales	£204,555	£197,455			
Direct materials	£39,000	£42,300			
Direct labour	£75,000	£83,000			
Production overheads	£69,000	£64,800			
Administration overheads	£53,000	£58,900			

127 TELMAH LTD

You have been provided with the following information about performance in the previous month.

Cost type	Budget £	Actual £	Variance £	Variance %	Significant/ not significant	Report to
Sales	310,000	353,400				
Fuel costs	25,000	31,250				
Entertaining	16,000	15,500				

Reporting policies state that:

- Variances in excess of 5% of budget and that are greater than £500 are significant. They should be reported to the department manager (DM).

- Adverse variances in excess of 10% of budget, and that are greater than £1,000 are significant. They should be reported to the department director (DD).

- Variances in excess of 20% of budget, and that are greater than £1,500 are significant. They should be reported to the department director (DD).

Complete the table above to show each variance and variance percentage. Identify whether each variance is significant or not and who (if anyone) the variance should be reported to.

PRACTICE QUESTIONS: SECTION 1

SPREADSHEETS

128 CELLS

Which ONE of the following is not one of the main aspects of formatting cells?

A   Wrapping text

B   Graphics

C   Setting number specification, e.g. working to two decimal places

D   Changing the font, size or colour of text

For the following questions you will need to access Excel files from MyKaplan. They are in the Excel Files section in Excel File: Exam Kit. You will be instructed when to use formulas.

129 DOOMSDAY LTD

Doomsday Ltd is costing its single product. You have been provided with budgeted information in a spreadsheet.

Complete the following table to calculate the total cost and unit cost for a production level of 20,000 units. Overheads are absorbed on a cost per unit basis.

(i)   Complete cells B9:C12, using formulas in cells B9, C9 and B12. Do NOT use spreadsheet formulas when entering your answers into cells B10:C11 and C12.

(ii) Format the total cost cells B9:B12 with a thousand separator, to the nearest whole pound

(iii) Format the unit cost cells C9:C12 to two decimal places

(iv) Make the contents of cells A12:C12 bold

(v)   Fill cell C12 with any colour.

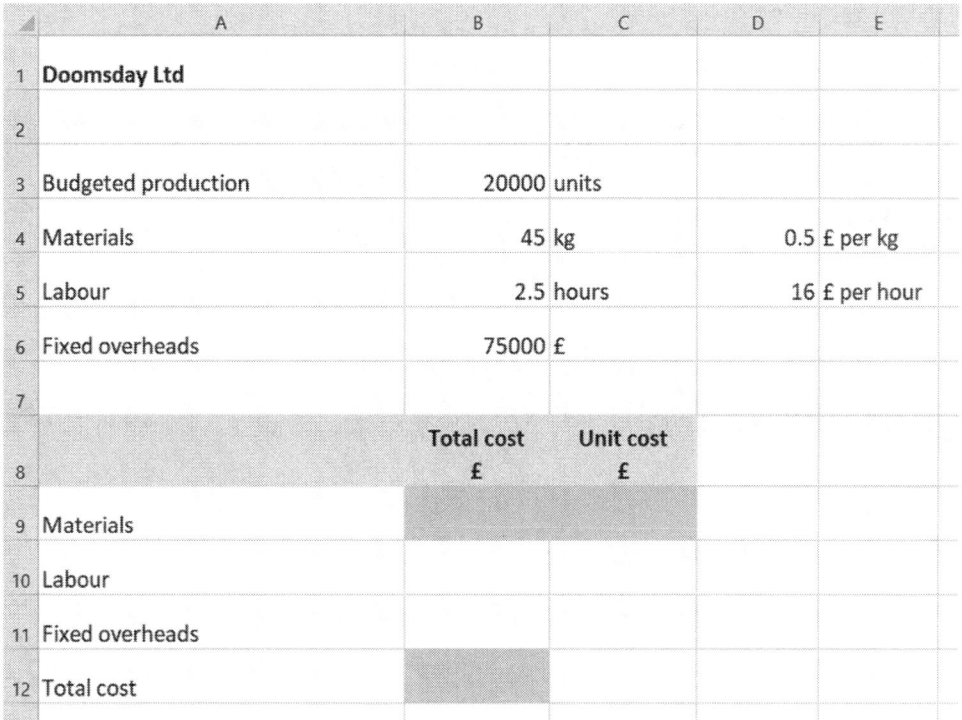

KAPLAN PUBLISHING   57

130 GRU LTD

Gru Ltd manufactures sheds and has collated cost information related to the month of June.

Complete the manufacturing account below for Gru Ltd below, ensuring that the headings are in the correct order of a manufacturing account.

(i) Select the correct headings from the drop-down list for the cells A6, A8, A10, A13 and A16

(ii) Calculate and insert the missing values in cells B6, B8, B10, B13 and B16. Do NOT use spreadsheet formulas when entering your answers.

(iii) Insert a new column to the left of column B

(iv) Merge and centre the title in A1 across cells A1:C1

(v) Place a border around the title cell.

	A	B
1	**Gru Ltd Manufacturing account**	
2		£
3	Opening inventory of raw materials	12,000
4	Puchases of raw materials	25,000
5	Closing inventory of raw materials	8,000
6		
7	Direct labour	22,000
8		
9	Manufacturing overheads	45,000
10		
11	Opening inventory of work in progress	13,500
12	Closing inventory of work in progress	17,000
13		
14	Opening inventory of finished goods	15,000
15	Closing inventory of finished goods	11,000
16		

131 HERB PLC

Herb plc makes a single product and for a production level of 20,000 units has the following cost details:

- Direct materials: 3 kgs per unit @ £18 per kg
- Direct labour: 1.5 hours @ £12 per hour
- Fixed overheads: £60,000

Complete the table below to show the unit cost at the production level of 20,000 units. Overheads are absorbed on a per labour hour basis.

(i) Insert 'Labour' into cell A5

(ii) Calculate and insert all missing values into cells B4:B7. Do NOT use spreadsheet formulas when entering your answers.

(iii) Calculate and enter the overhead absorption rate into cell B9. Do NOT use spreadsheet formulas when entering your answers.

(iv) Change the text size of cell A9 to 20

(v) Format cells B4:B7 and B9 to accounting, to two decimal places.

	A	B	C	D
1	Herb plc			
2				
3		Unit cost £		
4	Materials			
5				
6	Fixed overheads			
7	Total cost			
8				
9	Overhead absorption rate =		per labour hour	

AAT: **PRINCIPLES OF COSTING**

132 KAMILE LTD

Kamile Ltd has produced a spreadsheet detailing budgeted and actual costs for last month.

Reporting policies state that a variance is significant if it is in excess of 5% of budget.

(i) Using the information provided in cells A1:E5, complete the following table, cells B9:G12.

- Formulas MUST be used for figures entered into cells B9, B12, D9 and F9
- You MUST manually enter cell references. Do NOT enter any spaces into formula cells
- You should use standard round brackets, e.g. ( ), where relevant, in formulas
- The remaining cells should be completed by entering figures ONLY
- Show adverse variances using a minus sign (-)
- Monetary values should be to the nearest whole pound
- The variance % column has been preformatted to two decimal places

(ii) Identify whether the variances are adverse or favourable using the drop-down options in column E

(iii) Identify whether the variances are significant or not using the drop-down options in column G

	A	B	C	D	E	F	G
1	Kamile Ltd						
2							
3	Budgeted production	1500	units				
4	Sales revenue	250	£ per unit				
5	Material cost	4000	kgs		20	£ per kg	
6							
7							
8		Budget £ 1,500 units	Actual £ 1,500 units	Variance £	Adv/Fav	Variance %	Significant?
9	Revenue		390,000				
10	Materials		85,000				
11	Fixed overheads	45,000	43,000				
12	Profit / loss	−45,000	262,000	307,000		−682.22	

133 PHINEAS LTD

Phineas Ltd has produced a standard cost card for its only product and a spreadsheet detailing actual costs for last month.

(i) Using the information provided in cells A1:B11, complete the following table, cells B14:D18.

- Formulas MUST be used for figures entered into cells B16, B18, D15 and D18
- The formula in cell B18 must use both addition and subtraction
- You MUST manually enter cell references. Do NOT enter any spaces into formula cells
- You should use standard round brackets, e.g. ( ), where relevant, in formulas
- The remaining cells should be completed by entering figures ONLY
- Show adverse variances using a minus sign (-)
- Monetary values should be to the nearest whole pound

(ii) Identify whether the variances are adverse or favourable using the drop-down options in column E.

	A	B	C	D	E
1	Phineas Ltd				
2					
3	Budgeted production (units)	1200			
4					
5	**Cost card:**	£ per unit			
6					
7	Sales revenue	650			
8	Material	210			
9	Labour	168			
10	Fixed overheads	50			
11	Profit per unit	222			
12					
13		Budget £ 1,200 units	Actual £ 1,200 units	Variance £	Adv/Fav
14	Revenue		670,000		
15	Materials		248,000		
16	Labour		221,000		
17	Fixed overheads		58,000		
18	Profit / loss		143,000		

Section 2

ANSWERS TO PRACTICE QUESTIONS

COST CLASSIFICATION

FINANCIAL AND MANAGEMENT ACCOUNTING

1 FAMA

Characteristic	Financial accounting	Management accounting
• Have to be produced annually.	✓	
• Analyses historic events to help produce forecasts.		✓
• Is always produced using accounting standards.	✓	
• Is produced on an ad hoc basis when required.		✓

2 FINANCIAL AND MANAGEMENT

Characteristic	Financial accounting	Management accounting
• Must be presented as specified by the Companies Act and accounting standards.	✓	
• Helps managers run the business on a day-to-day basis.		✓
• Used as the basis for the calculation of the organisation's tax charge.	✓	
• Can include anything that managers feel is useful for the business.		✓

3 MAFA

Characteristic	Management accounting	Financial accounting
• It is based on past events.		✓
• Its purpose is to provide information for managers.	✓	
• It is based on future events.	✓	
• It complies with company law and accounting rules.		✓

4 FEATURES

Feature	Financial accounting	Management accounting
• Analysis of profit by cost centre.		✓
• Statement of profit or loss using format as dictated by accounting standards and company law.	✓	
• Cash flow forecasts.		✓
• Cost per unit calculation.		✓

RESPONSIBILITY CENTRES

5 MARIAM

	Cost centre	Profit centre
• Bakery	✓	
• Shop		✓
• Office	✓	

6 PRINT PLC

	Cost centre	Profit centre
• Binding		✓
• Shops		✓
• Marketing	✓	

7 HOOCH PLC

	Cost centre	Revenue centre	Profit centre	Investment centre
• Hooch's manager has no responsibility for income or asset purchases and disposals.	✓			
• Hooch's manager is assessed on the profitability of their department, as well as how effectively they have controlled their assets.				✓
• Hooch's manager is responsible for income and expenditure of their department only.			✓	
• Hooch's manager is responsible for income only.		✓		

8 SWING PLC

	Cost centre	Revenue centre	Profit centre	Investment centre
• HR department.	✓			
• A subsidiary company of a large corporation which makes its own capital investment decisions.				✓
• Sales department responsible only for meeting sales targets.		✓		
• Individual restaurant in a large chain.			✓	

CLASSIFYING COSTS BY ELEMENT (MATERIALS, LABOUR OR OVERHEADS)

9 VVV LTD

Cost	Materials	Labour	Overheads
• Paint used on the planes.	✓		
• Depreciation of the machines used in the factory.			✓
• Oil used on the machines in the factory.	✓		
• Salary of worker assembling the planes.		✓	

10 TRIP LTD

Cost	Materials	Labour	Overheads
• Wages of the insurance clerks dealing with claims.		✓	
• Rent of the office.			✓
• Paper used to print off insurance policies.	✓		
• Salary of the office manager.		✓	

11 FRUWT LTD

Cost	Materials	Labour	Overheads
• Purchase of fruit for juicing.	✓		
• Electricity used by juicing machines.			✓
• Water added to the juice before sale.	✓		
• Wages of staff operating juicing machinery.		✓	

12 MARTINA

Cost	Materials	Labour	Overheads
• Stationery used in Martina's court cases.	✓		
• Wages of Martina's secretary.		✓	
• Water rates for Martina's office.			✓
• Cost of training courses taken by Martina.			✓

ANSWERS TO PRACTICE QUESTIONS: SECTION 2

CLASSIFYING COSTS BY NATURE (DIRECT OR INDIRECT)

13 KHALED

Cost	Direct	Indirect
• Paper used in the newspapers.	✓	
• Wages of warehouse staff.		✓
• Heat and light for head office.		✓
• Ink used in printing the newspapers.	✓	

14 RUSSETT LTD

Cost	Direct	Indirect
• Glass used to make tablets.	✓	
• Insurance of factory.		✓
• Wages of workers assembling tablets.	✓	
• Cost of entertaining corporate clients.		✓

15 SCOTLAND LTD

Cost	Direct	Indirect
• Cleaners' wages.		✓
• Advertising expense.		✓
• Material used in production.	✓	
• Production manager's wages.		✓
• Machinist wages.	✓	

16 DIRECT OR INDIRECT

Cost	Direct	Indirect
• Chargeable hour for a lawyer.	✓	
• Machine hire for a building contractor in a long term contract.	✓	
• Electricity for a garden centre.		✓
• Audit fee for a restaurant.		✓

17 DIRECT COSTS

B

Direct costs are variable and are therefore usually assumed to be constant, regardless of the level of activity within the relevant range. Answer A is incorrect because it describes the behaviour of a fixed cost within the relevant range of activity. Answer C also describes a fixed cost, since the same total fixed cost would be shared over a varying number of units, resulting in a unit cost that varies with changes in activity levels. Answer D is incorrect because total variable costs are conventionally deemed to remain unaltered when activity levels remain constant.

CLASSIFYING COSTS BY FUNCTION (PRODUCTION, ADMINISTRATION OR SELLING AND DISTRIBUTION)

18 NOOGLE LTD

Cost	Production	Administration	Selling and distribution
• Purchases of plastic for ready meal containers.	✓		
• Depreciation of sales department's delivery lorries.			✓
• Insurance of office computers.		✓	
• Salaries of production workers.	✓		

19 HEAVING LTD

Cost	Production	Administration	Selling and distribution
• Paper used to print off sales invoices.		✓	
• Metal used to make weights and bars.	✓		
• Depreciation of sales person's vehicle.			✓
• Repairs to machine in factory.	✓		

20 KORMA PLC

Cost	Production	Administration	Selling and distribution	Finance
• Direct materials.	✓			
• Sales director's salary.			✓	
• Head office printer ink.		✓		
• Direct labour.	✓			
• Bank charges.				✓

21 PETAR

Cost	Production	Administration	Selling and distribution	Finance
• Salary of receptionist.		✓		
• Plastic used in false teeth.	✓			
• Stationery provided to all departments.		✓		
• Interest on Petar's bank overdraft.				✓
• Electricity for Petar's factory.	✓			

CLASSIFYING COSTS BY BEHAVIOUR (FIXED, VARIABLE OR SEMI-VARIABLE)

22 QUARK LTD

Cost	Fixed	Variable	Semi-variable
• Bar manager's salary.	✓		
• Alcohol used to make drinks.		✓	
• Rent of bar.	✓		
• Telephone costs, including standard line rental charge.			✓

23 MORN LTD

Cost	Fixed	Variable	Semi-variable
• Wood used in production.		✓	
• Advertising manager's salary.	✓		
• Electricity costs which include a standing charge.			✓
• Labour costs paid on a piecework basis.		✓	

24 STEPPED FIXED COST

A

A supervisor's wages are usually classified as a stepped cost because a supervisor may be responsible for supervising up to a specific number of workers. However, if output increases such that additional direct labour is required, then an extra supervisor will be required. For example,

1 – 10 workers   1 supervisor

11 – 20 workers   2 supervisors

25 BRAETAK LTD

Cost	Fixed	Variable	Semi-variable
• Rent of an office building.	✓		
• Wages of production staff paid on an hourly basis.		✓	
• Wages of production staff paid by a piece rate method.		✓	
• Sales staff paid a basic wage plus commission for each unit sold.			✓

Note: the piece rate scheme does not mention a guaranteed minimum wage so the correct answer is variable.

26 ODO LTD

Cost	Fixed	Variable	Semi-variable
• Material used in the production process.		✓	
• Safety review fee for the year.	✓		
• Electricity costs which include a standing charge.			✓
• Labour paid on a per unit basis.		✓	

27 DEFINITIONS

Behaviour	Fixed	Variable	Semi-variable	Stepped cost
• This type of cost increases in direct proportion to the amount of units produced.		✓		
• This type of cost has a fixed and a variable element.			✓	
• This type of cost remains constant despite changes in output.	✓			
• This type of cost is fixed within a certain range of output.				✓

28 MATCH A GRAPH

(a) Variable cost per unit – graph 1

(b) Total fixed cost – graph 1

(c) Stepped fixed costs – graph 3

(d) Total variable cost – graph 2

(e) Semi-variable cost – graph 4

ANSWERS TO PRACTICE QUESTIONS: **SECTION 2**

COST CODING

29 BYTES LTD

Cost	Code
• Salary of trainee IT consultant.	• B100
• Planning costs to renew lease of the office.	• C200
• Wages of the office manager.	• B200
• Cleaning materials used by cleaner.	• A200

30 HERO LTD

Transaction	Code
• Cost of major advertising campaign.	• 760/340
• Oil for machine in factory.	• 225/115
• Silk used in manufacturing of costumes.	• 225/110
• Insurance of head office.	• 485/230
• Sale of women's costumes to a supermarket chain.	• 115/085
• Wages paid to delivery van drivers.	• 760/340

31 VILLAIN LTD

Transaction	Code
• Petrol used to run drilling machinery.	• 015/200
• Sale of silver to a jewellery manufacturer.	• 011/200
• Replacement of worn out drilling machinery parts.	• 015/200
• Depreciation of fleet of delivery lorries.	• 024/200
• Salary of finance director.	• 019/200
• Sale of gold to an electronics company.	• 011/100

32 NAYULZ LTD

Cost	Code
• Income earned from salons in New York City, America.	RE228
• Bank loans raised to open a new store in London.	IN100
• Nail polish purchased for use in salon.	CO315
• Heat and light for salon.	CO325
• Nayulz funds invested in new project.	IN110

KAPLAN PUBLISHING

33 JUMPER LTD

Sale	Code
• Sale of one jumper to Ms. Wool	KNI/315
• Sale of protective trousers to a factory in London.	TRS/635
• Sale of large coats to an office in Birmingham.	MCN/515
• Sale of three hundred trousers to a shop in Manchester.	TRS/425

34 GREENFINGERS

Cost	Code
• Purchase of seeds used to grow plants for resale.	CS880
• External loans for investment in new greenhouses.	IN515
• Wages of gardeners who maintain the plants to be sold.	CS890
• Sales of food and drink.	RV795

COST BEHAVIOUR

CALCULATION QUESTIONS

35 HULK PLC

Statement	Fixed	Variable	Semi-variable
• Costs are £37,500 when 7,500 units are made and £62,500 when 12,500 units are made.		✓	
• Costs are £2 per unit when 7,500 units are made and £1.20 per unit when 12,500 units are made.	✓		
• Costs are £50,000 when 7,500 units are made and £80,000 when 12,500 units are made.			✓

£37,500 ÷ 7,500 units = £5 per unit; £62,500 ÷ 12,500 units = £5 per unit. Unit cost is constant therefore this is a variable cost.

7,500 units × £2 = £15,000; 12,500 units × £1.20 = £15,000. Total cost is constant at all activity levels therefore this is a fixed cost.

£50,000 ÷ 7,500 units = £6.67 £80,000 ÷ 12,500 units = £6.40. Unit cost not constant and so this is not a variable cost. Total cost is also not constant and so this is not a fixed cost. It therefore must be a **semi-variable** cost.

ANSWERS TO PRACTICE QUESTIONS: **SECTION 2**

36 BANNER PLC

Statement	Fixed	Variable	Semi-variable
• Costs are £5,000 plus £45 per unit, regardless of the number of units made.			✓
• Costs are £5,000 when 300 units are made and £5,000 when 600 units are made.	✓		
• Costs are £35 per unit regardless of the number of units made.		✓	

37 NORTON PLC

Statement	Fixed	Variable	Semi-variable
• Costs are £50,000 in total regardless of the number of units made.	✓		
• Costs are £50,000 in total when 2,500 units are made and £80,000 when 4,000 units are made.		✓	
• Costs are £7 per unit when 1,000 units are made and £6 per unit when 2,000 units are made.			✓

Note: The third cost must be semi-variable as it cannot be fixed (it changes as the number of units changes) and it cannot be purely variable as the cost per unit changes at different levels of activity.

38 TRIUMPH LTD

Statement	Fixed	Variable	Semi-variable
At 9,000 units this cost is £29,250, and at 12,000 units it is £39,000		✓	
At 5,000 units this cost is £5.20 per unit, and at 8,000 units it is £3.25 per unit	✓		
At 19,800 units, this cost is £64,500, and at 27,000 units it is £82,500			✓

£29,250 ÷ 9,000 units = £3.25, £39,000 ÷ 12,000 units = £3.25, therefore variable cost

5,000 units × £5.20 = £26,000, 8,000 units × £3.25 = £26,000, therefore fixed cost

£64,500 ÷ 19,800 units = £3.26, £82,500 ÷ 27,000 units = £3.06, therefore must be a **semi-variable** cost – it cannot be fixed (it changes as the number of units changes) and it cannot be purely variable as the cost per unit changes at different levels of activity.

39 YOUNGS LTD

	8,000 units	10,000 units	16,000 units
Variable cost (£)	40,000	50,000	80,000
Fixed cost (£)	30,000	30,000	30,000
Total cost (£)	70,000	80,000	110,000
Unit cost (£)	8.75	8.00	6.88

Variable cost per unit = £50,000/10,000 units = £5.00 per unit.

Variable cost at 8,000 units = £5.00 × 8,000 units = £40,000. At 16,000 units = £5.00 × 16,000 units = £80,000.

Fixed costs remain constant at £30,000 for all activity levels.

Total cost = variable cost + fixed costs, e.g. at 8,000 units = £40,000 + £30,000 = £70,000.

Unit cost = total cost/number of units, e.g. at 8,000 units = £70,000/8,000 = £8.75.

40 CARE PLC

	3,000 units	9,000 units	12,000 units
Variable cost (£)	12,600	37,800	50,400
Fixed cost (£)	12,000	12,000	12,000
Total cost (£)	24,600	49,800	62,400
Unit cost (£)	8.20	5.53	5.20

Workings for 3,000 units:

Variable cost per unit = £37,800/9,000 units = £4.20 per unit. Total variable cost = £4.20 × 3,000 units = £12,600.

Fixed costs remain constant at £12,000 for all activity levels.

Total cost = variable cost + fixed costs = £12,600 + £12,000 = £24,600.

Unit cost = total cost/number of units = £24,600/3,000 units = £8.20 per unit.

Same principles apply for 12,000 units.

41 ROBSHAW LTD

	9,000 units	11,000 units	16,500 units
Variable cost (£)	22,500	27,500	41,250
Fixed cost (£)	35,000	35,000	35,000
Total cost (£)	57,500	62,500	76,250
Unit cost (£)	6.39	5.68	4.62

Workings for 11,000 units:

Variable cost per unit = £22,500/9,000 units = £2.50 per unit. Total variable cost = £2.50 × 11,000 units = £27,500.

Fixed costs remain constant at £35,000 for all activity levels.

Total cost = variable cost + fixed costs = £27,500 + £35,000 = £62,500.

Unit cost = total cost/number of units = £62,500/11,000 units = £5.68 per unit.

Same principles apply for 16,500 units.

ANSWERS TO PRACTICE QUESTIONS: SECTION 2

NARRATIVE STYLE QUESTIONS

42 BUNGLE LTD

Statement	True	False
• Total variable costs will decrease.		✓
• Total fixed costs will remain the same.	✓	
• The variable cost per unit will remain the same.	✓	
• The fixed cost per unit will increase.		✓

43 TF

Statement	True	False
• Variable costs change directly with changes in activity.	✓	
• Fixed costs change directly with changes in activity.		✓
• Stepped costs are fixed within a set range of output.	✓	

44 FIXED OR VARIABLE

Cost	Fixed	Variable
• Direct materials.		✓
• Power used in production machinery.		✓
• Training costs for new employees in production.	✓	
• Insurance for sales cars.	✓	
• Insurance machinery.	✓	
• Sales commission.		✓

45 FOV

Cost	Fixed	Variable
• Piecework wages paid to factory workers.		✓
• Salaries paid to company directors.	✓	
• Annual payment for cleaning of air conditioning units.	✓	

46 VOF

Cost	Fixed	Variable
• Annual salaries paid to factory managers.	✓	
• Hourly wages paid to factory workers.		✓
• Colour ink used to print magazines.		✓

47 STORM

Cost	Overhead?	
	Yes	No
• Labour cost of workers who assemble the product.		✓
• Insurance cost of factory where product is assembled.	✓	
• Heat and light for manufacturing machines.	✓	

48 ROGUE

Cost	Overhead?	
	Yes	No
• Labour cost of cleaning staff in a factory.	✓	
• Depreciation of delivery vans.	✓	
• Cost of materials used to build the product.		✓

49 GAMBIT

Cost	Overhead?	
	Yes	No
• Wages of staff paid on a piecework system.		✓
• Cost of factory canteen staff hourly wages.	✓	
• Direct materials.		✓

ANSWERS TO PRACTICE QUESTIONS: SECTION 2

COST CARDS, TOTAL COSTS AND UNIT COSTS

50 JEEPERS LTD

Cost	Direct	Indirect
• Materials used in production.	✓	
• Piecework labour costs.	✓	
• Salary of chief executive.		✓

Element	Unit product cost
Materials (W1)	£35
Labour (W2)	£8
Direct cost (materials + labour)	£43
Overheads (W3)	£38
Total	£81

(W1) Total material cost for 15,000 units = 37,500kilos × £14 = £525,000

Material cost per unit = £525,000/15,000 = £35

(W2) Total labour cost for 15,000 units = 7,500 hours × £16 = £120,000

Labour cost per unit = £120,000/15,000 = £8

(W3) Overhead per unit = £570,000/15,000 = £38

51 BRANIAC LTD

Element	Unit cost
Materials	£24.50
Labour	£40.25
Direct cost	£64.75
Overheads	£12.50
Total	£77.25

52 MARKO LTD

	Unit cost	Total cost for 20,000 units
Variable production costs	£5.50	£110,000
Fixed production costs	£4.00	£80,000
Total production cost	£9.50	£190,000

KAPLAN PUBLISHING

53 BIZARRO LTD

Element	Unit cost	Total cost
Materials	£45.00	£765,000
Labour	£9.00	£153,000
Overheads	£2.50	£42,500
Total	£56.50	£960,500

54 VINNY LTD

	Unit cost	Total cost
Materials	£5	**£75,000**
Labour	**£8** (W1)	**£120,000**
Direct costs	**£13** (W2)	**£195,000**
Overheads	**£6.67** (W3)	£100,000
Total cost	£19.67	£295,000

(W1) Total labour cost for 15,000 units = £120,000. Cost per unit = £120,000/15,000 = £8

(W2) Direct costs per unit = direct materials + direct labour = £5 + £8 = £13

(W3) Overhead per unit = £100,000/15,000 units = £6.67

55 DARKSEID LTD

Element	Unit cost
Materials	£3.50 (W1)
Labour	£6.75 (W2)
Fixed overheads	£2.42 (W3)
Total	£12.67

(W1) Total material cost for 95,000 units = 47,500kg × £7 = £332,500

Material cost per unit = £332,500/95,000 = £3.50

(W2) Total labour cost for 95,000 units = 71,250 hrs × £9 = £641,250

Labour cost per unit = £641,250/95,000 = £6.75

(W3) Fixed overheads total does not change. The revised cost per unit is £242,000/100,000 = £2.42

56 OLSEN LTD

Element	Unit cost
Materials	£12.00
Labour	£17.00
Direct cost	£29.00
Production overheads	£1.00
Total cost per unit	£30.00

57 FLAKEWAY LTD

Element	Unit cost
Materials	£5.00
Labour	**£4.00** (W1)
Direct cost	£9.00
Overheads	**£2.00** (W2)
Total	£11.00

(W1) Total labour cost = 8,000 hours × £12 per hour = £96,000. Labour per unit = £96,000/24,000 units = £4.

(W2) Overhead cost per unit = £48,000/24,000 units = £2.

58 CORONATION LTD

	Total cost for 5,000 units
Direct costs	£32,500
Production overhead	£40,000
Non production overhead	£45,000
Total costs	£117,500

59 LUTHOR LTD

Element	Unit cost
Materials	£60.00
Labour	£22.50
Fixed overheads	£38.00
Total	£120.50

AAT: PRINCIPLES OF COSTING

OVERHEAD ABSORPTION

60 WILKINSON LTD

(a)

	Machine hour	Labour hour	Unit
Overheads (£)	150,000	150,000	150,000
Activity	10,000	12,500	60,000
Absorption rate (£)	15.00	12.00	2.50

(b)

Cost	Machine hour (£)	Labour hour (£)	Unit (£)
Material	10.00	10.00	10.00
Labour	2.50	2.50	2.50
Direct cost	12.50	12.50	12.50
Overheads	2.50 (W1)	3.00 (W2)	2.50 (W3)
Total unit cost	15.00	15.50	15.00

(W1) Each unit requires 10 minutes of production time (or 10/60 hour). The OAR for machine time is £15.00 per hour. Therefore the overhead absorbed will be 10/60 × £15.00 = £2.50.

(W2) Each unit requires 15 minutes of labour time (or 15/60 hour). The OAR for labour time is £12.00 per hour. Therefore the overhead absorbed will be 15/60 × £12.00 = £3.

(W3) Each unit will absorb the same flat unit rate of £2.50 per unit.

61 HODGSON LTD

(a)

	Machine hour	Labour hour	Unit
Overheads (£)	250,000	250,000	250,000
Activity	15,000	20,000	100,000
Absorption rate (£)	16.67	12.50	2.50

(b)

Cost	Machine hour (£)	Labour hour (£)	Unit (£)
Material	24.00	24.00	24.00
Labour	6.00	6.00	6.00
Direct cost	30.00	30.00	30.00
Overheads	5.56	6.25	2.50
Total unit cost	35.56	36.25	32.50

62 BARNES LTD

	Machine hour	Labour hour	Unit
No. hours/units	17,500	12,000	40,000
Hours per unit	0.4375	0.30	
Absorption rate (£)	£7.43	£10.83	£3.25
Overhead per unit (£)	£3.25	£3.25	£3.25

63 MAJA LTD

	Machine hour	Labour hour	Unit
No. hours/units	9,000	11,000	60,000
Hours per unit	0.15	0.1833	
Absorption rate (£)	£16.11	£13.18	£2.42
Overhead per unit (£)	£2.42	£2.42	£2.42

AAT: PRINCIPLES OF COSTING

MANUFACTURING ACCOUNTS

64   JOKER LTD

Manufacturing account – Y/E 31 December

	£
Opening inventory of raw materials	50,000
Purchases of raw materials	120,000
Closing inventory of raw materials	65,000
DIRECT MATERIALS USED	
Direct labour	140,000
DIRECT COST	
Manufacturing overheads	85,000
MANUFACTURING COST	
Opening inventory of work in progress	48,000
Closing inventory of work in progress	52,000
COST OF GOODS MANUFACTURED	
Opening inventory of finished goods	57,000
Closing inventory of finished goods	61,000
COST OF GOODS SOLD	

	£
DIRECT MATERIALS USED	105,000 (W1)
DIRECT COST	245,000 (W2)
MANUFACTURING COST	330,000 (W3)
COST OF GOODS MANUFACTURED	326,000 (W4)
COST OF GOODS SOLD	322,000 (W5)

(W1) Direct materials used = purchases of raw materials + opening raw material inventory – closing raw material inventory = 120,000 + 50,000 – 65,000 = 105,000

(W2) Direct cost = direct materials + direct labour cost = 105,000 (W1) + 140,000 = 245,000

(W3) Manufacturing cost = direct cost + indirect cost of manufacture = 245,000 + 85,000 = 330,000

(W4) Cost of goods manufactured = manufacturing cost + opening inventory of work in progress – closing inventory of work in progress = 330,000 + 48,000 – 52,000 = 326,000

(W5) Cost of goods sold = cost of goods manufactured + opening inventory finished goods – closing inventory finished goods = 326,000 + 57,000 – 61,000 = 322,000

65 TUT LTD

	£
Opening inventory of raw materials	10,000
Purchases of raw materials	60,000
Closing inventory of raw materials	12,000
DIRECT MATERIALS USED	**58,000** (W1)
Direct labour	88,000
DIRECT COST	**146,000** (W2)
Manufacturing overheads	45,000
MANUFACTURING COST	**191,000** (W3)
Opening inventory of work in progress	12,000
Closing inventory of work in progress	15,000
COST OF GOODS MANUFACTURED	**188,000** (W4)
Opening inventory of finished goods	18,000
Closing inventory of finished goods	20,000
COST OF GOODS SOLD	**186,000** (W5)

(W1) Direct materials used = purchases of raw materials + opening raw material inventory – closing raw material inventory = 60,000 + 10,000 – 12,000 = 58,000

(W2) Direct cost = direct materials + direct labour cost = 58,000 (W1) + 88,000 = 146,000

(W3) Manufacturing cost = direct cost + indirect cost of manufacture = 146,000 + 45,000 = 191,000

(W4) Cost of goods manufactured = manufacturing cost + opening inventory of work in progress – closing inventory of work in progress = 191,000 + 12,000 – 15,000 = 188,000

(W5) Cost of goods sold = cost of goods manufactured + opening inventory finished goods – closing inventory finished goods = 188,000 + 18,000 – 20,000 = 186,000

66 RIDDLER LTD

	£
Direct cost	292,000 (W1)
Manufacturing overhead	112,000 (W2)
Total manufacturing cost	404,000 (W3)
Cost of goods manufactured	400,000 (W4)
Cost of goods sold	410,000 (W5)

(W1) Direct cost = direct material cost + direct labour cost = 98,000 (see below) + 194,000

Direct material cost = purchases of raw materials + opening raw material inventory − closing raw material inventory = 100,000 + 20,000 − 22,000 = 98,000

(W2) Manufacturing overhead = indirect materials + indirect labour cost + factory indirect expenses = 25,000 + 12,000 + 75,000 = 112,000

(W3) Manufacturing cost = direct cost + manufacturing overheads = 292,000 + 112,000 = 404,000

(W4) Cost of goods manufactured = manufacturing cost + opening inventory of work in progress − closing inventory of work in progress = 404,000 + 31,000 − 35,000 = 400,000

(W5) Cost of goods sold = cost of goods manufactured + opening inventory finished goods − closing inventory finished goods = 400,000 + 60,000 − 50,000 = 410,000

67 CLOCKING LTD

	£
Prime cost	144,000 (W1)
Manufacturing overhead	71,000 (W2)
Total manufacturing cost	215,000 (W3)
Cost of goods manufactured	213,000 (W4)
Cost of goods sold	218,000 (W5)

(W1) Direct cost = direct material cost + direct labour cost = 47,000 (see below) + 97,000

Direct material cost = purchases of raw materials + opening raw material inventory − closing raw material inventory = 50,000 + 7,000 − 10,000 = 47,000

(W2) Manufacturing overhead = indirect materials + indirect labour cost + factory indirect expenses = 8,000 + 10,000 + 53,000 = 71,000

(W3) Manufacturing cost = direct cost + manufacturing overheads = 144,000 + 71,000 = 215,000

(W4) Cost of goods manufactured = manufacturing cost + opening inventory of work in progress − closing inventory of work in progress = 215,000 + 8,000 − 10,000 = 213,000

(W5) Cost of goods sold = cost of goods manufactured + opening inventory finished goods − closing inventory finished goods = 213,000 + 30,000 − 25,000 = 218,000

68 BOOKWORM LTD

	£
Direct materials used	12,000 (W1)
Direct cost	27,000 (W2)
Manufacturing cost	52,000 (W3)
Cost of goods manufactured	50,000 (W4)
Cost of goods sold	46,000 (W5)

(W1) Direct materials used = opening inventory of raw materials + purchases of raw materials – closing inventory of raw materials = 5,000 + 15,000 – 8,000 = 12,000

(W2) Direct cost = direct material cost + direct labour cost = 12,000 + 15,000 = 27,000

(W3) Manufacturing cost = direct cost + manufacturing overheads = 27,000 + 25,000 = 52,000

(W4) Cost of goods manufactured = manufacturing cost + opening inventory of work in progress – closing inventory of work in progress = 52,000 + 4,000 – 6,000 = 50,000

(W5) Cost of goods sold = cost of goods manufactured + opening inventory finished goods – closing inventory finished goods = 50,000 + 12,000 – 16,000 = 46,000

69 MULTI

C – Manufacturing cost + opening WIP – closing WIP + opening FG – closing FG

COSTING FOR INVENTORY AND WORK-IN-PROGRESS

NARRATIVE STYLE QUESTIONS

70 BOBBLE LTD

Characteristic	
• Potentially out of date valuation of inventory issues.	FIFO
• The valuation of inventory rarely reflects the actual purchase price of the material.	AVCO
• Potentially out of date closing inventory valuation.	LIFO

71 LINT LTD

Statement	True	False
• In periods of rising prices, FIFO gives a higher valuation of closing inventory than LIFO or AVCO.	✓	
• In periods of falling prices, LIFO gives a higher valuation of issues of inventory than FIFO or AVCO.		✓
• AVCO would normally be expected to produce a valuation of closing inventory somewhere between valuations under FIFO and LIFO.	✓	

72 FLUFF LTD

Characteristic	FIFO	LIFO	AVCO
• This inventory valuation method is particularly suited to inventory that consist of liquid materials e.g. oil.			✓
• This inventory valuation method is suited to inventory that has a short shelf life e.g. dairy products.	✓		
• This inventory valuation method is suited to a wheat farmer who has large silos of grain. Grain is added to and taken from the top of these silos.		✓	

73 FIDO LTD

Characteristic	FIFO	LIFO	AVCO
• In times of rising prices this method will give higher profits.	✓		
• In times of rising prices this method will give lower profits.		✓	
• In times of rising prices this method gives a middle level of profits compared to the other two.			✓

74 TRUFFEAUX LTD

Statement	True	False
• FIFO costs issues of inventory at the most recent purchase price.		✓
• AVCO costs issues of inventory at the oldest purchase price.		✓
• LIFO costs issues of inventory at the oldest purchase price.		✓
• FIFO values closing inventory at the most recent purchase price.	✓	
• LIFO values closing inventory at the most recent purchase price.		✓
• AVCO values closing inventory at the latest purchase price.		✓

75 STOCKY LTD

Characteristic	FIFO	LIFO	AVCO
• Issues are valued at the most recent purchase cost.		✓	
• Inventory is valued at the average of the cost of purchases.			✓
• Inventory is valued at the most recent purchase cost.	✓		

ANSWERS TO PRACTICE QUESTIONS: SECTION 2

76 BUFFER

	TRUE	FALSE
• Holding costs per unit of inventory would increase	✓	
• Average inventory levels would reduce		✓

77 INVENTORY

	TRUE	FALSE
• Inventory levels will increase		✓
• Inventory holding costs will increase	✓	

IDENTIFICATION OF INVENTORY VALUATION METHOD

78 EPIC LTD

(a)

Characteristic	
• Closing inventory is valued at £28,200.	AVCO
• The issue of inventory is valued at £67,000.	FIFO
• The issue of inventory is valued at £64,000.	LIFO

(b)

	True	False
• AVCO values the issue of inventory at £65,800.	✓	
• LIFO values the closing inventory at £27,000.		✓
• FIFO values the closing inventory at £30,000.		✓

Using FIFO:

Issues will be made from the oldest inventories first. This is the 8,000 units @ £5 per unit (8,000 × £5 = £40,000).

The remaining issue of 6,000 units will be made from the purchase of 12,000 units. This will be 6,000 units @ £4.50 (6,000 × £4.50 = £27,000).

The total issue will be valued at £40,000+£27,000 = £67,000.

The closing inventory will be the remainder of the purchase in the month, which is 6,000 (12,000 – 6,000) units @ £4.50 = £27,000.

Using LIFO:

Issues will be made from the most recent purchase first. This is the 12,000 units @ £4.50 per unit (12,000 × £4.50 = £54,000).

The remaining issue of 2,000 units will be made from the opening inventory valued at £5. This will be 2,000 units @ £5 (2,000 × £5 = £10,000).

The total issue will be valued at £54,000 + £10,000 = £64,000.

The closing inventory will be the remainder of the opening inventory, which is 6,000 units @ £5 = £30,000.

Using AVCO:

The value of the inventory will be averaged. The total number of units is 20,000 units (8,000 + 12,000). The total cost is (8,000 × £5) + (12,000 × £4.50) = £94,000.

The average cost per unit is therefore £94,000/20,000 = £4.70.

The value of the issue will therefore be 14,000 × £4.70 = £65,800.

The closing inventory will also be valued at this average, which will be 6,000 × £4.70 = £28,200.

79 AWESOME LTD

(a)

Characteristic	
• Closing inventory is valued at £48,500.	FIFO
• The issue of inventory is valued at £57,200.	AVCO
• The issue of inventory is valued at £66,900.	LIFO

(b)

	True	False
• FIFO values the issue of inventory at £47,500.	✓	
• AVCO values the closing inventory at £38,400.		✓
• LIFO values the closing inventory at £29,100.	✓	

80 AMAZING LTD

(a)

Characteristic	FIFO	LIFO	AVCO
• Closing inventory is valued at £1,500.		✓	
• The issue of inventory is valued at £23,000.	✓		
• The issue of inventory is valued at £24,000.			✓

(b)

	True	False
• LIFO values the issue of inventory at £26,500.	✓	
• AVCO values the closing inventory at £5,000.		✓
• FIFO values the closing inventory at £4,000.		✓

Using FIFO:

Issues will be made from the oldest inventories first. This is the 2,000 units @ £1.50 per unit (2,000 × £1.50 = £3,000).

The remaining issue of 4,000 units will be made from the purchase of 5,000 units. This will be 4,000 units @ £5 (4,000 × £5 = £20,000).

The total issue will be valued at £3,000 + £20,000 = £23,000.

The closing inventory will be the remainder of the purchase in the month, which is 1,000 (5,000-4,000) units @ £5 = £5,000.

Using LIFO:

Issues will be made from the most recent purchase first. This is the 5,000 units @ £5 per unit (5,000 × £5 = £25,000).

The remaining issue of 1,000 units will be made from the opening inventory valued at £1.50. This will be 1,000 units @ £1.50 (1,000 × £1.50 = £1,500).

The total issue will be valued at £25,000 + £1,500 = £26,500.

The closing inventory will be the remainder of the opening inventory, which is 1,000 units @ £1.50 = £1,500.

Using AVCO:

The value of the inventory will be averaged. The total number of units is 7,000 units (2,000 + 5,000). The total cost is (2,000 × £1.50) + (5,000 × £5) = £28,000.

The average cost per unit is therefore £28,000/7,000 = £4.

The value of the issue will therefore be 6,000 × £4 = £24,000.

The closing inventory will also be valued at this average, which will be 1,000 × £4 = £4,000.

AAT: PRINCIPLES OF COSTING

INVENTORY CARDS

81 STONE LTD

Method	Cost of issue on 22 June	Closing inventory at 30 June
FIFO	£10,125 (500 × £15) + (150 × £17.50)	£17,200 (£8,750 + £4,950 + £6,125 + £7,500) − £10,125
LIFO	£11,450 (275 × £18) + (350 × £17.50) + (25 × £15)	£15,875 (£8,750 + £4,950 + £6,125 + £7,500) − £11,450
AVCO	£10,732 ((£7,500 + £6,125 + £4,950)/ (500 + 350 + 275)) × 650	£16,593 (£8,750 + £4,950 + £6,125 + £7,500) − £10,732

82 NATAL LTD

(a)

Method	Cost of issue on 2 Dec	Closing inventory at 29 Dec
LIFO	£534,250 (50,000 × £7) + (14,000 × £8) + (8500 × £8.50)	£42,750 (£85,000 + £112,000 + £350,000 + £30,000) − £534,250
AVCO	£535,912 ((£85,000 + £112,000 + £350,000)/ (10,000 + 14,000 + 50,000)) × 72,500	£41,088 (£85,000 + £112,000 + £350,000 + £30,000) − £535,912

(b)

	True	False
• FIFO would give a lower closing inventory valuation on the 29th December than LIFO and AVCO.	✓	
• FIFO would give a lower cost of issue on the 25th of December than LIFO and AVCO.		✓

83 GANDALF LTD

	Valuation £
• July 15	£1,030 (500 × £1.70) + (120 × £1.50)
• July 31	£660 (200 × £1.80) + (200 × £1.50)

84 GRUNDY LTD

Method	Cost of issue on 25 October	Closing inventory at 31 October
FIFO	£20,000 (6000 × £2.50) + (2500 × £2)	£5,500
LIFO	£15,250 (3000 × £1) + (3000 × £2) + (2500 × £2.50)	£10,250
AVCO	£17,000 (AVCO = £24,000/12000 units = £2/unit Cost of issue = 8500 × £2)	£8,500

Tutorial note

The quickest way to calculate closing inventory is as total purchases (£25,500) less cost of issues.

85 LOBO LTD

Method	Cost of issue on 29 May	Closing inventory at 30 May
FIFO	£2,500 (250 × £5.50) + (250 × £4.50)	£2,250
LIFO	£1,000 (500 × £2)	£3,750
AVCO	£1,750 (AVCO = £4,375/1,250 = £3.50/unit, giving cost of issue of 500 × £3.50)	£3,000

Tutorial note

Quickest to calculate closing inventory as total purchases (£4,750) less cost of issue

86 ZOD LTD

Tutorial note

This question is harder than those seen in the sample assessment but is here to give you more of a challenge!

Method	Cost of issue on 16 Feb	Closing inventory at 26 Feb
FIFO	£290	£905
AVCO (see working below)	£255	£924

AVCO Workings:

DATE	RECEIPTS		ISSUES		BALANCE		
	Units	Cost	Units	Cost	Units	Unit cost	Total cost
February 2	100	£500			100	£5	£500
February 3			50		**(50)**	**(£5)**	**(£250)**
					50	£5	£250
February 12	150	£600			**150**	**£4**	**£600**
					200	£4.25	£850
February 16			60		**(60)**	**(£4.25)**	**(£255)**
					140	(£4.25)	£595
February 20	110	£505			**110**	£4.59 (to nearest penny)	**£505**
					250	£4.40	£1,100
February 26			40		**(40)**	**(£4.40)**	**(£176)**
					210	4.40	£924

ANSWERS TO PRACTICE QUESTIONS: SECTION 2

COSTING FOR LABOUR

NARRATIVE STYLE QUESTIONS

87 NULAB LTD

Payment method	Time-rate	Piecework	Piece-rate plus bonus
• Labour is paid based on the production achieved.		✓	
• Labour is paid extra if an agreed level of output is exceeded.			✓
• Labour is paid according to hours worked.	✓		

88 LU LTD

Payment method	Time-rate	Piecework	Time-rate plus bonus
• Assured level of remuneration for employee.	✓		
• Employee earns more if they work more efficiently than expected.		✓	
• Assured level of remuneration and reward for working efficiently.			✓

89 MANDELA LTD

Statement	True	False
• Time rate is paid based on the production achieved.		✓
• Overtime is paid for hours worked over the standard hours agreed.	✓	
• Piece rate is paid according to hours worked.		✓

90 PERRES LTD

Payment method	Overtime rate
• This is the amount paid above the basic rate for hours worked in excess of the normal hours.	Overtime premium
• This is the total amount paid per hour for hours worked in excess of the normal hours.	Overtime rate
• This is the amount paid per hour for normal hours worked.	Basic rate

91 TEVEZ LTD

Statement	True	False
• Direct labour costs can be identified with the goods being made or the service being provided.	✓	
• Indirect labour costs vary directly with the level of activity.		✓

92 BERDYCH LTD

Payment method	Variable	Fixed
• Labour that is paid based on a time rate basis per hour worked.	✓	
• Labour is paid on a monthly salary basis.		✓
• Labour that is based on number of units produced.	✓	

93 SODERLING LTD

Payment method	Salary
• Assured level of remuneration for employee usually agreed for the year.	SALARY
• Employee earnings are directly linked with units they produce.	PIECEWORK
• Employee earnings are directly linked with hours they work.	TIME-RATE

94 MURRAY LTD

	True	False
• Indirect labour costs includes production supervisors' salaries.	✓	
• Direct labour costs usually vary directly with the level of activity.	✓	

95 OLGA LTD

Payment method	Time-rate	Piecework	Salary
• Employee is paid the same amount every month.			✓
• Employee wage increases in direct correlation with the number of hours worked.	✓		
• Employee wage increases in direct correlation with the number of units produced.		✓	

ANSWERS TO PRACTICE QUESTIONS: SECTION 2

96 PIECEWORK STATEMENTS

Statement	True	False
• Piecework encourages employees to work harder.	✓	
• Piecework requires accurate recording of the number of hours staff have worked.		✓
• Piecework encourages workers to improve the quality of the units they produce.		✓

CALCULATING LABOUR COSTS

97 MUTANT LTD

Worker	Hours worked	Basic wage	Overtime	Gross wage
S. Torm (W1)	34 hours	£240	£23	£263
J. Grey (W2)	38 hours	£240	£68	£308

(W1) Basic wage is based on 32 hour week = 32 × £7.50 = £240

Overtime is paid at time and a half (£7.50 × 1.5 = £11.25) = (34-32) hours × £11.25 = £23

(W1) Basic wage is based on 32 hour week = 32 × £7.50 = £240

Overtime is paid at time and a half (£7.50 × 1.5 = £11.25) = (38-32) hours × £11.25 = £68

98 PHOENIX LTD

Statement	True	False
An employee who works 38 hours and makes 775 units will not receive a bonus. (W1)		✓
An employee who works 40 hours and makes 815 units will receive total pay of £342.50. (W2)	✓	
An employee who works 37 hours and makes 744 units will earn a bonus of £6. (W3)	✓	

(W1) In 38 hours a worker should make 38 × 20 = 760 units. If a worker made 775 units, this is 15 units above the expectation, and so a bonus would be paid.

(W2) In 40 hours a worker should make 40 × 20 = 800 units. If a worker made 815 units, this is 15 units above the expectation. The bonus will therefore be 15 × £1.50 = £22.50. The basic wage will be 40 hours @ £8 = £320. The total pay will therefore be £320 + £22.50 = £342.50.

(W3) In 37 hours a worker should make 37 × 20 = 740 units. If a worker made 744 units, this is 4 units above the expectation. The bonus will therefore be 4 × £1.50 = £6.

AAT: PRINCIPLES OF COSTING

99 KAHN LTD

Worker	Hours worked	Units produced	Basic wage	Bonus	Gross wage
A. Smith (W1)	35	175	£420	£0	£420
J. O'Hara (W2)	35	180	£420	£6	£426
M. Stizgt (W3)	35	185	£420	£12	£432

(W1) In 35 hours a worker should make 35 × 5 = 175 units. No bonus will be paid.

(W2) In 35 hours a worker should make 35 × 5 = 175 units. If 180 units are made, this is 5 units above expectation. If 5 units can be made in 1 hour this is equivalent to 1 hour's work. The bonus will therefore be 1 × £6 = £6.

(W3) If a worker made 185 units, this is 10 units above the expectation. If 5 units can be made in 1 hour this is equivalent to 2 hour's work. The bonus will therefore be 2 × £6 = £12.

100 ENTERPRISE LTD

Bonus calculation	Correct	Incorrect
Javier produced 400 units and earned a bonus of £6. (W1)		✓
Esha produced 465 units and earned a bonus of £390. (W2)		✓
Mika produced 480 units and earned a bonus of £300. (W3)	✓	

(W1) The bonus is paid for every unit in excess of 400 units, therefore beginning at unit 401. No bonus will be paid for the 400th unit.

(W2) If 465 units are produced, this is 65 more than the target. However, the bonus is capped at 450 units. Therefore the bonus will only be received for units 401–450 (i.e. 50 units). The maximum bonus achievable is therefore 50 × £6 = £300.

(W3) If 480 units are produced, this is 80 more than the target. However, the bonus is capped at 450 units. Therefore the bonus will only be received for units 401–450 (i.e. 50 units). The maximum bonus achievable is therefore 50 × £6 = £300.

101 SGC LTD

Worker	Units produced in week	Gross wage
J. O'Neill	500 units	£660.00 (W1)
S. Carter	650 units	£772.50 (W2)

(W1) Basic salary = £285. If 500 units are produced this will be paid at £0.75 × 500 = £375. Gross wage = £285 + £375 = £660.

(W2) Basic salary = £285. If 650 units are produced this will be paid at £0.75 × 650 = £487.50. Gross wage = £285 + £487.50 = £772.50.

ANSWERS TO PRACTICE QUESTIONS: SECTION 2

102 GOTHIC LTD

Pay calculation	Correct	Incorrect
M. Shelley worked for 35 hours and earned total income of £595. (W1)		✓
G. Leroux worked for 37 hours and earned total income of £929.	✓	
A.E. Poe worked for 32 hours and earned total income of £874.		✓
The total bonus paid by Gothic Ltd was £1,500.	✓	

Production target = 20,000 units. Actual output = 22,100 units. This is an increase of 2,100 units, with a percentage increase of 2,100/20,000 × 100 = 10.5% (therefore 10 complete percent). The bonus will therefore be 10 × £30 = £300 for each employee.

(W1) Basic wage = 35 × £17 = £595. Plus bonus of £300 = £895.

(W2) Basic wage = 37 × £17 = £629. Plus bonus of £300 = 929.

(W3) Basic wage = 32 × £17 = £544. Plus bonus of £300 = 844.

(W4) Total bonus = £300 × 5 employees = £1,500.

103 AVENGERS LTD

Worker	Hours worked	Basic wage	Overtime	Gross wage
T. Stark	138	£1,380	£0	£1,380
B. Banner	142	£1,400	£25	£1,425
S. Rogers	145	£1,400	£63	£1,463

104 DRACO LTD

Worker	Units produced in week	Gross wage
P. Jones	240 units	£192 (W1)
D. Bannatyne	350 units	£250 (W2)
L. Redford	250 units	£200 (W3)

(W1) No units produced above standard, therefore all are paid at £0.80 (240 × £0.80 = £192).

(W2) 100 units above standard are made (350-250). These are paid a bonus of £10 per 20 units. This is therefore a bonus of 100/20 × £10 = £50. Standard production is all paid at £0.80 which is therefore £0.80 × 250 = £200. Gross wage = £200 + £50 = £250.

(W3) No units above the standard are made. The bonus does not start until unit 251. Standard production is all paid at £0.80 which is therefore £0.80 × 250 = £200.

AAT: PRINCIPLES OF COSTING

105 QUAGGA PLC

Statement	True	False
During a 29 hour week, an employee producing 1,475 units would not receive a bonus.		✓
During a 32 hour week, an employee producing 1,665 units would receive a bonus of £29.25.	✓	
During a 37 hour week, an employee producing 1,925 units would receive total pay of £300.25.		✓

106 JLA PLC

Statement	True	False
During a 30 hour week, an employee producing 192 units would receive a bonus of £16.	✓	
During a 35 hour week, an employee producing 240 units would receive total pay of £215.	✓	
During a 30 hour week, an employee producing 180 units would not receive a bonus.	✓	

107 INJUSTICE LTD

Worker	Units produced	Basic wage	Piece work	Gross wage
N. Wing	295	£175	£354	£529
W. Woman	355	£175	£426	£601
T. Flash	385	£175	£462	£637

108 GREENWOOD LTD

Worker	Hours worked	Units produced	Basic wage	Bonus	Gross wage
B. Ryan	35	175	£350	£0	£350
S. Chang	35	190	£350	£21	£371
E. Schneider	35	210	£350	£49	£399

109 SANCHO LTD

Worker	Hours worked	Units produced	Basic wage	Bonus	Gross wage
A. Ali	38	115	£630	£180	£810
B. Jiou	33	100	£630	£180	£810
C. Perry	35	94	£630	£180	£810

Total units produced = 115 + 100 + 94 = 309. Bonus units produced = 309 − 300 = 9 units

Bonus per team member = 9 units × £20 per unit = £180

ANSWERS TO PRACTICE QUESTIONS: **SECTION 2**

BUDGETING AND VARIANCES

NARRATIVE QUESTIONS

110 PIERRE LTD

Statement	True	False
Fixed budgets are prepared at the start of a budget period and are not adjusted to reflect changes during the period	✓	
Flexible budgets can be prepared at the start of the budget period and can be adjusted to reflect changes in activity level during the period	✓	

111 NIXON LTD

Statement	True	False
One of the purposes of a budget is to ensure that production levels are coordinated with expected sales levels	✓	
One of the purposes of budgets is to ensure that staff are aware that all responsibilities are carried out by senior management		✓

112 VARIOUS LTD

Statement	True	False
• A variance is the difference between budgeted and actual cost.	✓	
• A favourable variance means actual costs are less than budgeted.	✓	
• An adverse variance means that actual income is less than budgeted.	✓	
• A favourable variance occurs when actual income is the same as budgeted income.		✓

113 NOOR LTD

Statement	True	False
If budgeted sales are 6,000 units at £7.50 per unit and actual sales are £47,600, the sales variance is favourable (W1)	✓	
A favourable cost variance occurs when an actual cost of £9,800 is compared to a budgeted cost of £24 per unit for a budgeted output of 400 units (W2)		✓
A variance arises from a comparison of budgeted costs for last year with actual costs for this year		✓
If actual material costs are the same as budgeted costs for materials then no variance arises	✓	

(W1) Sales variance = actual sales – budgeted sales = £47,600 – (6,000 × £7.50) = £2,600.

As actual sales are greater than budgeted, the income will be greater, and the variance is favourable.

(W2) If budgeted costs for 400 units are £24 each, this is a total budget of £9,600. If actual costs are £9,800 then this means we have incurred more costs than planned. This is therefore an adverse variance as profits will be reduced.

114 GATLAND LTD

Statement	True	False
If budgeted sales are 4,000 units at £9.50 per unit and actual sales are £35,200, the sales variance is favourable		✓
A favourable cost variance occurs when an actual cost of £6,400 is compared to a budgeted cost of £14 per unit for a budgeted output of 500 units	✓	
A variance arises from a comparison of budgeted costs for last year with budgeted costs for this year		✓
If actual material costs are the same as budgeted costs for materials then the materials variance is adverse		✓

(W1) Sales variance = actual sales – budgeted sales = £35,200 – (4,000 × £9.50) = (£2,800).

As actual sales are less than budgeted, the income will be lower, and the variance is adverse.

(W2) If budgeted costs for 500 units are £14 each, this is a total budget of £7,000. If actual costs are £6,400 then this means we have incurred less costs than planned. This is therefore a favourable variance as profits will be increased.

ANSWERS TO PRACTICE QUESTIONS: SECTION 2

115 LANCASTER LTD

Statement	True	False
If budgeted sales are 14,000 units at £3.50 per unit and actual sales are £45,200, the sales variance is favourable		✓
An adverse cost variance occurs when an actual cost of £68,400 is compared to a budgeted cost of £14 per unit for a budgeted output of 5,000 units		✓
A variance arises from a comparison of budgeted costs for this year with actual costs for this year	✓	
If actual material costs are the same as budgeted costs for materials then the materials variance is favourable		✓

116 GOODE LTD

Statement	True	False
The variance for the Direct Material cost of Department B should be reported to the purchasing manager	✓	
The variance for the Direct Labour cost for Department A should be reported to the sales manager		✓
The variance for the Direct Labour cost for Department B should be reported to the production manager of Department A		✓
A Direct Material cost variance that has been deemed Not Significant should not be reported	✓	

117 BROWN LTD

Statement	True	False
The variance for the Direct Material cost of Department A should be reported to the purchasing manager	✓	
The variance for the Direct Labour cost for Department A should be reported to the production manager of Department B		✓
The variance for sales should be reported to the sales manager	✓	
A Direct Material cost variance that has been deemed Significant should not be reported		✓

118 MAGENTA LTD

Statement	True	False
An increase in the production workers' hourly rate of pay could result in an adverse labour variance	✓	
An increase in the efficiency of the production workers could result in an adverse labour variance		✓

AAT: PRINCIPLES OF COSTING

119 CARLOTA LTD

Statement	True	False
Increasing the selling price per unit might result in a favourable sales variance	✓	
Increased competition from rival companies might result in a favourable sales variance		✓

CALCULATION QUESTIONS

120 FUNKY LTD

	Budget £ 3,000 units
Sales revenue	270,000 (W1)
Direct materials	60,000 (W2)
Direct labour	36,000 (W3)
Fixed overhead	40,000
Profit/loss	134,000

(W1) Sales revenue = 3,000 units × £90 = £270,000

(W2) Direct materials = 3,000 units × 2kg per unit × £10 per kg = £60,000

(W3) Direct labour = 3,000 units × 2 hours per unit × £6 per hour = £36,000

121 EREBOR LTD

Cost type	Budget £	Actual £	Variance £	Adverse or favourable (A or F)
Sales	600,500	597,800	2,700	A
Direct materials	205,800	208,500	2,700	A
Direct labour	155,000	154,800	200	F
Production overheads	65,000	72,100	7,100	A
Administration overheads	58,400	55,200	3,200	F

122 MORIA LTD

Cost type	Budget	Variance	Variance as % of budget	Significant or Not significant
Sales	45,100	4,214	9 (W1)	S
Material	15,750	1,260	8 (W2)	S
Labour	12,915	805	6	NS
Variable overheads	5,750	315	5	NS
Fixed overheads	8,155	1,011	12	S

(W1) Variance as % = variance/budget × 100 = 4,214/45,100 × 100 = 9 %

(W2) Variance as % = variance/budget × 100 = 1,260/15,750 × 100 = 8 %

123 WYEDALE LTD

Cost type	Budget £	Actual £	Variance £	Variance %	Adverse/ Favourable
Sales	27,000	29,775	2,775	10	F
Direct materials	7,400	8,510	1,110	15	A
Direct labour	7,200	7,920	720	10	A
Production overheads	5,500	5,390	110	2	F
Administration overheads	4,500	4,365	135	3	F

Variance as % = variance/budget × 100

124 BELEGOST LTD

	Budget £	Actual £	Adverse or Favourable (A or F)	Significant or Not significant (S or NS)
Sales	205,000	207,100	F	NS
Direct materials	75,150	78,750	A	NS
Direct labour	110,556	107,950	F	NS
Production overheads	14,190	12,500	F	S
Non-production overheads	16,190	17,880	A	S

Variance as % = variance/budget × 100

125 IVAN LTD

	Budget £	Actual £	Variance £	Adverse or Favourable
Sales	540,000 (W1)	547,450	7,450	Favourable
Direct materials	50,000 (W2)	80,200	30,200	Adverse
Direct labour	125,000 (W3)	146,000	21,000	Adverse
Fixed overheads	120,000	144,200	24,200	Adverse
Profit/loss	245,000	177,050	67,950	Adverse

(W1) Sales = 20,000 × £27 per unit = £540,000

(W2) Direct materials = 20,000 units × 5 kg per unit × £0.50 per kg = £50,000

(W3) Direct labour = 20,000 units × 0.25 hours per unit × £25 per hour = £125,000

Cost type	Budget £	Actual £	Variance £	Adverse or favourable (A or F)
Sales	544,750	547,450	2,700	F
Direct materials	76,800	80,200	3,400	A
Direct labour	148,400	146,000	2,400	F
Production overheads	136,000	144,200	8,200	A
Administration overheads	105,000	109,800	4,800	A

126 BLUEBELL LTD

Cost type	Budget £	Actual £	Variance £	Adv/ Fav	%
Sales	£204,555	£197,455	7,100	A	3
Direct materials	£39,000	£42,300	3,300	A	8
Direct labour	£75,000	£83,000	8,000	A	11
Production overheads	£69,000	£64,800	4,200	F	6
Administration overheads	£53,000	£58,900	5,900	A	11

127 TELMAH LTD

Cost type	Budget £	Actual £	Variance £	Variance %	Significant/ not significant	Report to
Sales (W1)	310,000	353,400	43,400	14.00	S	DM
Fuel costs (W2)	25,000	31,250	6,250	25.00	S	DD
Entertaining (W3)	16,000	15,500	500	3.13	NS	–

(W1) Sales variance = 353,400 – 310,000 = 43,400.

Percentage variance = 43,400/310,000 × 100 = 14%. This is a favourable variance and so bullet point 2 does not apply. It is less than 20% and so bullet point 3 does not apply. It is greater than 5% and greater than £500 and so is significant and should be reported to the department manager.

(W2) Fuel costs variance = 31,250 – 25,000 = 6,250.

Percentage variance = 6,250/31,250 × 100 = 25%. This is an adverse variance and bullet points 2 and 3 apply and so is significant. It should therefore be reported to the department director.

(W3) Entertaining variance = 15,500 – 16,000 = 500.

Percentage variance = 500/16,000 × 100 = 3.13%. This is a favourable variance and so bullet point 2 does not apply. It is less than 20% and so bullet point 3 does not apply. It is greater than 5%, but less than £500 and so is not significant and does not need to be reported to anyone.

SPREADSHEETS

128 CELLS

B. Graphics are not part of formatting cells.

For the following answers you can also access them as Excel files from MyKaplan. They are in the Excel Files section in Excel File: Exam Kit

129 DOOMSDAY LTD

	A	B	C	D	E
1	**Doomsday Ltd**				
2					
3	Budgeted production	20000	units		
4	Materials	45	kg	0.5	£ per kg
5	Labour	2.5	hours	16	£ per hour
6	Fixed overheads	75000	£		
7					
8		Total cost £	Unit cost £		
9	Materials	450,000	22.50		
10	Labour	800,000	40.00		
11	Fixed overheads	75,000	3.75		
12	Total cost	1,325,000	66.25		

Formula:

	A	B	C	
8		Total cost £	Unit cost £	
9	Materials	=B3*B4*D4	=B4*D4	← Could also be =B9/B3
10	Labour	800000	40	
11	Fixed overheads	75000	3.75	
12	Total cost	=SUM(B9:B11)	66.25	

130 GRU LTD

A	B	C
Gru Ltd Manufacturing account		
		£
Opening inventory of raw materials		12,000
Puchases of raw materials		25,000
Closing inventory of raw materials		8,000
DIRECT MATERIALS USED		29,000
Direct labour		22,000
DIRECT COST		51,000
Manufacturing overheads		45,000
MANUFACTURNG COST		96,000
Opening inventory of work in progress		13,500
Closing inventory of work in progress		17,000
COST OF GOODS MANUFACTURED		92,500
Opening inventory of finished goods		15,000
Closing inventory of finished goods		11,000
COST OF GOODS SOLD		96,500

131 HERB PLC

	A	B	C	D
1	Herb plc			
2				
3		Unit cost £		
4	Materials	£ 54.00		
5	Labour	£ 18.00		
6	Fixed overheads	£ 3.00		
7	Total cost	£ 75.00		
8				
9				
10	Overhead absorption rate =	£ 2.00	per labour hour	

Materials cost = 3kg × £18 per kg = £54

Labour cost = 1.5 hours × £12 = £18

Overhead per unit = 1.5 hours × £2.00 per hour (W1) = £3.00

(W1) Overhead absorption rate = overheads/number of labour hours (W2) = £60,000/30,000 = £2.00 per labour hour.

(W2) Total number of labour hours = 20,000 units × 1.5 hours per unit = 30,000 hours.

132 KAMILE LTD

	A	B	C	D	E	F	G
1	Kamile Ltd						
2							
3	Budgeted production	1500	units				
4	Sales revenue	250	£ per unit				
5	Material cost	4000	kgs		20	£ per kg	
6							
7							
8		Budget £ 1,500 units	Actual £ 1,500 units	Variance £	Adv/Fav	Variance %	Significant?
9	Revenue	375,000	390,000	15,000	Favourable	4.00	No
10	Materials	80,000	85,000	-5,000	Adverse	-6.25	Yes
11	Fixed overheads	45,000	43,000	2,000	Favourable	4.44	No
12	Profit / loss	250,000	262,000	12,000	Favourable	4.80	No

Formula:

		Budget £ 1,500 units	Actual £ 1,500 units	Variance £	Adv/Fav	Variance %	Significant?
8							
9	Revenue	=B4*B3	390000	=C9-B9	Favourable	=D9/B9*100	No
10	Materials	=B5*D5	85000	-5000	Adverse	-6.25	Yes
11	Fixed overheads	45000	43000	2000	Favourable	4.44	No
12	Profit / loss	250000	262000	12000	Favourable	4.8	No

133 PHINEAS LTD

	A	B	C	D	E
1	**Phineas Ltd**				
2					
3	Budgeted production (units)	1200			
4					
5	**Cost card:**	£ per unit			
6					
7	Sales revenue	650			
8	Material	210			
9	Labour	168			
10	Fixed overheads	50			
11	Profit per unit	222			
12					
13		Budget £ 1,200 units	Actual £ 1,200 units	Variance £	Adv/Fav
14	Revenue	780,000	670,000	-110,000	Adverse
15	Materials	252,000	248,000	4,000	Favourable
16	Labour	201,600	221,000	-19,400	Adverse
17	Fixed overheads	60,000	58,000	2,000	Favourable
18	Profit / loss	266,400	143,000	-123,400	Adverse
19					

Formula:

		Budget £ 1,200 units	Actual £ 1,200 units	Variance £	Adv/Fav
13					
14	Revenue	780000	670000	-110000	Adverse
15	Materials	252000	248000	=B15-C15	Favourable
16	Labour	=B9*B3	221000	-19400	Adverse
17	Fixed overheads	60000	58000	2000	Favourable
18	Profit / loss	=B14-SUM(B15:B17)	143000	=C18-B18	Adverse

Section 3

MOCK – QUESTIONS

TASK 1 (8 MARKS)

This task is about classification and relationship of costs.

(a) Identify whether the following statements are true or false.

Statement	True	False
Management accounts may be presented in any format required by managers.		
Financial accounts are prepared using historical cost information.		
Financial accounts will contain future forecasts.		

(3 marks)

(b) Identify the nature of the following costs.

Cost	Direct	Indirect
Chargeble hour for an accountancy practice.		
Premises insurance for a restaurant.		
Chief Executive's salary.		
Purchase of shampoo for a haridressers.		

(4 marks)

(c) Complete the following sentence.

Costs where the average cost per unit is constant at any activity level, are known as ☐

Options:

| variable costs. |
| fixed costs. |

(1 mark)

KAPLAN PUBLISHING 111

TASK 2 (10 MARKS)

This task is about costing techniques.

Juma Ltd is costing its single product which has the following cost details:

Variable costs	Per unit	Cost
Materials	3kg	£10 / kg
Labour	1.75 hours	£22 / hour

Overheads are absorbed on a per unit basis.

(a) **Complete the following table showing the total cost and unit cost for a production level of 6,000 units. Enter unit cost values to two decimal places and total cost to the nearest whole pound.**

Element	Unit cost £	Total cost £
Materials		
Labour		
Overheads		60,000
Total cost		

(5 marks)

(b) **Identify whether the following statements relate to planning, control or decision making.**

Statement	
Helping management with monitoring performance.	
Helping management to plan labour needs.	
Helping management to set unit sales prices.	

(3 marks)

(c) **Identify whether the following statements related to labour costing methods are true or false.**

Statement	True	False
Businesses paying using the time-rate method must offer overtime.		
Direct labour is never salaried.		

(2 marks)

TASK 3 (8 MARKS)

This task is about recording costs.

Wellgone Ltd, a firm of consultants, uses an alphanumeric coding system to allocate costs, as follows.

Activity	Code	Sub-class	Sub code
Revenue	REV	IT consultancy	100
		HR consultancy	200
Consultancy costs	CON	Wages	100
		Admin support	200
Marketing	MAR	Telephone	324
		Wages	345

(a) Code the following transactions for the project, using the table above. Each transaction should have a six character code.

Transaction	Code
Marketing telephone costs	
HR consultancy sales	

(2 marks)

(b) Identify whether the following statements relating to coding systems are true or false.

Statement	True	False
Coding systems facilitate data processing.		
It is not possible to add new codes after the initial system has been set up.		

(2 marks)

(c) Identify whether the following costs would be classified as product or period costs.

Cost	Product	Period
Manufacturing supplies.		
Sales and marketing expenses.		
Finance charges on a company's bank loans.		
Direct labour costs.		

(4 marks)

TASK 4 (10 MARKS)

This task is about calculating overhead absorption rates and looking at the behaviour of costs.

(a) **Identify the correct cost behaviour for the following costs.**

Cost behaviour	Fixed	Variable	Semi-variable	Step-fixed
The cost is fixed for a limited output range and then increases.				
The unit cost is the same whatever the output level.				
The cost consists of a part that stays the same and a part that changes with the output level.				
The total cost is the same whatever the output level				

(4 marks)

Frodo Ltd is considering how to cost the various products it makes. It needs to decide on the overhead absorption basis it will use.

One of Frodo Ltd's products is the Komodo. Each unit of the Komodo requires 30 minutes of machine time and 45 minutes of labour time.

(b) **Complete the table below to show the three overhead absorption rates that Frodo Ltd could use and what the overhead cost per unit of the Komodo would be using the three different overhead absorption rates. Enter all values to two decimal places.**

	Machine hour	Labour hour	Unit
Overheads (£)	180,000	180,000	180,000
Activity	26,866	45,000	60,000
Absorption rate (£)			
Overhead cost per unit (£)			

(6 marks)

TASK 5 (12 MARKS)

This task is about calculating costs of products and using tools and techniques to improve presentation.

Garcia Ltd has the following cost information for its last quarter.

	£
Materials costs:	
Materials forming part of the product	36,000
Materials not forming part of the product	4,000
Labour costs:	
Labour working on production	10,000
Labour supporting work on production	34,000
Other factory indirect expenses	26,000

Relevant inventory changes were as below.

	£
Work in progress:	
Opening	3,000
Closing	12,000
Finished goods:	
Opening	14,000
Closing	12,000

(a) Use the information provided to complete Garcia's cost structure below for the last quarter.

   (i) Calculate the values in cells B2:B6. Do NOT use spreadsheet formulas when entering your answers

   (ii) Insert 'Manufacturing cost' into cell A4

   (iii) Format cells B2:B6 as 'Accounting' to nil decimal places

   (iv) Place any border around cells A1:B6

   (v) Format cells A6 and B6 in bold

	A	B
1	**Garcia Ltd Manufacturing Account**	£
2	Direct materials used	
3	Direct cost	
4		
5	Cost of goods manufactured	
6	Cost of goods sold	

(12 marks: 8 – accounting, 4 – spreadsheets)

TASK 6 (12 MARKS)

This task is about labour and inventory calculations.

Fandom Ltd has made the following purchases and issues of raw material SL4 during the first half of April.

1 April   purchased 3,000 kg at £1.50 per kg

10 April   purchased 12,000 kg at £1.80 per kg

25 April   issued 10,800 kg to production

27 April   purchased 9,600 kg at £2.00 per kg

(a) (i) Complete the table below showing the cost of the issue of SL4 on 25 April. Enter values to the nearest whole pound.

Method	Cost of issue £
FIFO	
LIFO	
AVCO	

(3 marks)

(ii) Identify if the following changes to inventory contol policy are likely to increase or decrease Fandom Ltd's storage costs.

	Reduce	Increase
Making smaller, more frequent purchase orders.		
Inceasing the buffer stock level.		

(2 marks)

A company pays its employees a basic rate of £12 per hour for a 35 hour working week.

Any overtime is paid at time and a half.

(b) (i) Complete the table below for the two employees working the hours as shown. Enter all values to two decimal places. If no overtime is paid to an employee, you should enter '0' in the relevant field.

	Hours worked	Basic wage £	Overtime premium £	Gross pay £
Employee 1	39			
Employee 2	35			

(4 marks)

The company has a production target of 400 units for each production employee. Any excess production is rewarded by a bonus of £6 per unit, capped at a maximum production of 450 units.

(ii) **Identify whether the bonus calculations for the following employees are correct or incorrect.**

Bonus calculation	Correct	Incorrect
Employee 3 produces 400 units and earns a bonus of £6.		
Employee 4 produces 420 units and earns a bonus of £120.		
Employee 5 produces 460 units and earns a bonus of £360.		

(3 marks)

TASK 7 (20 MARKS)

This task is about budget calculations and exception reporting using formulas.

(a) **Identify whether the following statements about the use of budgets are true or false.**

	True	False
Fixed budgets are the most useful for making comparisons against actual results for control purposes.		
Budgets provide a benchmark against which managers can compare actual performance.		

(2 marks)

Number Crunchers Ltd provides accountancy services, specialising in the completion of personal tax returns. In the month of June it expected to complete 150 tax returns, each one requiring two hours of an accountant's time.

Number Crunchers Ltd charges its clients £250 for each completed tax return and the cost of the accountant's time is charged to each job at £40 per hour.

Fixed overheads for the month are expected to be £8,000.

(b) (i) **Using the information above and in cells A1:B5, complete the following table, cells B9:E12.**

- Formulas MUST be used for figures entered into cells B9, B12, D9 and E11
- You MUST manually enter cell references. Do NOT enter any spaces into formula cells
- You should use standard round brackets, e.g. ( ), where relevant, in formulas
- The remaining cells should be completed by entering figures ONLY
- Show adverse variances using a minus sign (-)
- Monetary values should be to the nearest whole pound

(ii) Identify whether the variances are adverse or favourable using the dropdown lists in cells F9:F11.

	A	B	C	D	E	F
1	Number Crunchers Ltd June Budget					
2						
3	Budgeted number of returns	150				
4	Sales revenue (per tax return)	£ 250				
5	Labour cost (per hour)	£ 40				
6						
7						
8		Budget £ 150 units	Actual £ 150 units	Variance £	Variance %	Adv/Fav
9	Revenue		39,000			
10	Labour		14,000			
11	Fixed overheads		7,600			
12	Profit / loss		17,400			

(17 marks: 13 – accounting, 4 – spreadsheets)

(c) Identify whether the following would be most likely to result in an adverse or favourable variance.

	Adverse	Favourable
Receiving less income than budgeted in a period.		

(1 mark)

Section 4

MOCK – ANSWERS

TASK 1 (8 MARKS)

(a)

Statement	True	False
Management accounts may be presented in any format required by managers.	✓	
Financial accounts are prepared using historical cost information.	✓	
Financial accounts will contain future forecasts.		✓

(3 marks)

(b)

Cost	Direct	Indirect
Chargeble hour for an accountancy practice.	✓	
Premises insurance for a restaurant.		✓
Chief Executive's salary.		✓
Purchase of shampoo for a haridressers.	✓	

(4 marks)

(c)

Costs where the average cost per unit is constant at any activity level, are known as | variable costs

(1 mark)

AAT: PRINCIPLES OF COSTING

TASK 2 (10 MARKS)

(a)

Element	Unit cost £	Total cost £
Materials	**30.00**	**180,000**
Labour	**38.50**	**231,000**
Overheads	**10.00**	60,000
Total cost	78.50	471,000

(5 marks)

Workings:

Materials cost per unit = 3 kg × £10 per kg = £30.

Total materials cost = materials cost per unit × number of units = £30 × 6,000 = £180,000.

Labour cost per unit = 1.75 hours × £22 per hour = £38.50.

Total labour cost = labour cost per unit × number of units = £38.50 × 6,000 = £231,000.

Overhead cost per unit = total overheads / number of units = £60,000 / 6,000 = £10 per unit.

(b)

Statement	
Helping management with monitoring performance.	Control
Helping management to plan labour needs.	Planning
Helping management to set unit sales prices.	Decision making

(3 marks)

(c)

Statement	True	False
Businesses paying using the time-rate method must offer overtime.		✓
Direct labour is never salaried.		✓

(2 marks)

TASK 3 (8 MARKS)

(a)

Transaction	Code
Marketing telephone costs	MAR324
HR consultancy sales	REV200

(2 marks)

(b)

Statement	True	False
Coding systems facilitate data processing.	✓	
It is not possible to add new codes after the initial system has been set up.		✓

(2 marks)

(c)

Cost	Product	Period
Manufacturing supplies.	✓	
Sales and marketing expenses.		✓
Finance charges on a company's bank loans.		✓
Direct labour costs.	✓	

(4 marks)

TASK 4 (10 MARKS)

(a)

Cost behaviour	Fixed	Variable	Semi-variable	Step-fixed
The cost is fixed for a limited output range and then increases.				✓
The unit cost is the same whatever the output level.		✓		
The cost consists of a part that stays the same and a part that changes with the output level.			✓	
The total cost is the same whatever the output level	✓			

(4 marks)

(b)

	Machine hour	Labour hour	Unit
Overheads (£)	180,000	180,000	180,000
Activity	26,866	45,000	60,000
Absorption rate (£)	**6.70** (W1)	**4.00** (W2)	**3.00** (W3)
Overhead cost per unit (£)	**3.35** (W4)	**3.00** (W5)	**3.00**

(6 marks)

Workings:

(W1) Machine hour absorption rate = £180,000/26,866 hours = £6.70/hr

(W2) Labour hour absorption rate = £180,000/45,000 hours = £4.00/hr

(W3) Per unit absorption rate = £180,000/60,000 units = £3.00/ unit.

(W4) 30 minutes of machine time = 30/60 hours

Machine hour overhead = 30/60 × £6.70/hr = £3.35

(W5) 45 minutes of labour time = 45/60 hours

Labour hour overhead = 45/60 × £4.00/hr = £3.00

TASK 5 (12 MARKS)

(a)

	A	B
1	**Garcia Ltd Manufacturing Account**	£
2	Direct materials used	£ 36,000
3	Direct cost	£ 46,000
4	Manufacturing cost	£ 110,000
5	Cost of goods manufactured	£ 101,000
6	**Cost of goods sold**	£ 103,000

(12 marks: 8 – accounting, 4 – spreadsheets)

Workings:

Direct cost = direct materials used + direct labour = £36,000 + £10,000 = £46,000

Manufacturing cost = direct cost + manufacturing overheads = £46,000 + (£4,000 + £34,000 + £26,000) = £110,000

Cost of goods manufactured = manufacturing cost + opening WIP - closing WIP = £110,000 + £3,000 – £12,000 = £101,000

Cost of goods sold = cost of goods manufactured + opening finished goods - closing finished goods = £101,000 + £14,000 – £12,000 = £103,000

AAT: PRINCIPLES OF COSTING

TASK 6 (12 MARKS)

(a) (i)

Method	Cost of issue £
FIFO	**18,540** (W1)
LIFO	**19,440** (W2)
AVCO	**18,792** (W3)

(3 marks)

(W1) Issues made from the oldest inventory first, starting with the 3,000 kgs purchased on 1 April and the remaining 7,800 kg (10,800 − 3,000) from the purchase on 10 April:

	Cost per unit £	Total cost £
3,000 kgs on 1 April	1.50	4,500
7,800 litres on 10 April	1.80	14,040
10,800 kgs		18,540

(W2) Issues made from the newest inventory first, purchased on 10 April, at a cost of £1.80 per kg.

Cost of issue = 10,800 kg × £1.80 = £19,440.

(W3) Issues made at the average cost immediately before the issue was made.

$$\text{Average cost} = \frac{(3{,}000 \text{ kg} \times £1.50) + (12{,}000 \text{ kg} \times £1.80)}{3{,}000 \text{ kg} + 12{,}000 \text{ kg}} = \frac{£26{,}100}{15{,}000 \text{ kg}} = £1.74 \text{ per kg}$$

Cost of issue = 10,800 kg × £1.74 = £18,792.

(ii)

	Reduce	Increase
Making smaller, more frequent purchase orders.	✓	
Inceasing the buffer stock level.		✓

(2 marks)

Making smaller, more frequent orders will result in a lower level of inventory being held in the store room at any one time. This will reduce storage costs.

Increasing the buffer stock level will mean that there is more inventory held in the store room. This will increase the associated costs of storage.

(b) (i)

	Hours worked	Basic wage £	Overtime premium £	Gross pay £
Employee 1 (W1)	39	**468.00**	**24.00**	492.00
Employee 2 (W2)	35	**420.00**	**0**	420.00

(4 marks)

Workings:

(W1) Employee 1

Basic pay = 39 hours × £12 = £468

Overtime hours = 39 – 35 = 4 hours

Overtime premium = £12 × 50% = £6 per hour, for 4 hours = 4 × £6 = £24.

(W2) Employee 2

Basic pay = 35 hours × £12 = £420

Overtime = nil

(ii)

Bonus calculation	Correct	Incorrect
Employee 3 produces 400 units and earns a bonus of £6. (W1)		✓
Employee 4 produces 420 units and earns a bonus of £120. (W2)	✓	
Employee 5 produces 460 units and earns a bonus of £360. (W3)		✓

(3 marks)

Workings:

(W1) The bonus only starts to be paid for production in excess of 400 units. Therefore the first unit to receive the bonus will be unit 401. This calculation is therefore incorrect.

(W2) This employee has produced 20 excess units. Each will be paid at £6, resulting in a bonus of 20 × £6 = £120. This calculation is therefore correct.

(W3) This employee has produced 60 excess units. However, don't forget that the bonus is capped at production of 450 units, therefore the maximum bonus will be paid for 50 units. The bonus is therefore 50 units × £6 = £300. This calculation is therefore incorrect.

AAT: PRINCIPLES OF COSTING

TASK 7 (20 MARKS)

(a)

	True	False
Fixed budgets are the most useful for making comparisons against actual results for control purposes.		✓
Budgets provide a benchmark against which managers can compare actual performance.	✓	

(2 marks)

Flexible budgets are more useful for making comparisons of actual results for control purposes.

(b)

	A	B	C	D	E	F
1	Number Crunchers Ltd June Budget					
2						
3	Budgeted number of returns	150				
4	Sales revenue (per tax return)	£ 250				
5	Labour cost (per hour)	£ 40				
6						
7						
8		Budget £ 150 units	Actual £ 150 units	Variance £	Variance %	Adv/Fav
9	Revenue	37,500	39,000	1,500	4.00	Favourable
10	Labour	12,000	14,000	-2,000	-16.67	Adverse
11	Fixed overheads	8,000	7,600	400	5.00	Favourable
12	Profit / loss	17,500	17,400	-100	-0.57	Adverse

(17 marks: 13 – accounting, 4 – spreadsheets)

Workings:

		Budget £ 150 units	Actual £ 150 units	Variance £	Variance %	Adv/Fav
8						
9	Revenue	=B3*B4	39000	=C9-B9	4	Favourable
10	Labour	12000	14000	-2000	-16.666	Adverse
11	Fixed overheads	8000	7600	400	=D11/B11*100	Favourable
12	Profit / loss	=B9-SUM(B10:B11)	=C9-C10-C11	-100	-0.571	Adverse

(c)

	Adverse	Favourable
Receiving less income than budgeted in a period.	✓	

(1 mark)